THE TEENAGE SURVIVAL BOOK

by

Sol Gordon

Times
BOOKS

THE TEENAGE SURVIVAL BOOK is a revised edition of **YOU**

Library of Congress Cataloging in Publication Data

Gordon, Sol, 1923—
The teenage survival book.

Earlier ed. © 1975 published under title: You!
1. Adolescent psychology. 2. Identity (Psychology)
3. Interpersonal relations. 4. Success.
I. Title.
BF724.G64   1980   158'.1   80-5781
ISBN 0-8129-0972-0

CREDITS:

Woodcut, pg. 20 by Albrecht Durer; Drawing pg. 9 by Harvey Cohen: Photo pg. 56
by permission of the Library of Congress; Portrait of the author
pg. 144 by Rita Fecher.
MANUFACTURED IN THE UNITED STATES OF AMERICA.
468B975

THE
TEENAGE SURVIVAL
BOOK

Also by Sol Gordon

WHEN LIVING HURTS:
WHY LOVE IS NOT ENOUGH
LIFE'S UNCERTAIN...EAT DESSERT FIRST

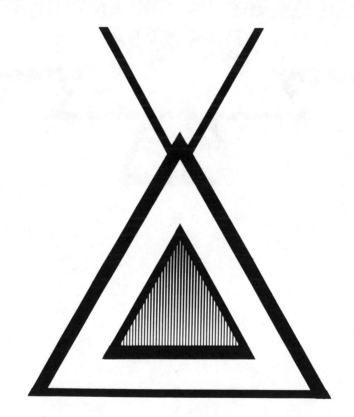

This edition is dedicated to
Phyllis Kaplan,
earth mother to thousands of young people
and to us

HOW IS THIS SELF-IMPROVEMENT BOOK DIFFERENT FROM OTHER SELF-IMPROVEMENT BOOKS?

Other self-improvement books tell you:

Not to worry. (When's the last time someone told you to stop
worrying and you stopped?)

Not to feel guilty. (If you've done something wrong, why shouldn't
you feel guilty?)

That you can be anything you want to be. (You should live so long.)

To get rid of unrealistic expectations. (How does one know in
advance that one's expectations are unrealistic?)

That if you eliminate shoulds, musts, perfectionistic tendencies,
worries, and other imperfections you'll be happy. (So, what else
is new?)

The plain fact is that:

Life, in large part, is made up of things to worry about

not only personal things

but the state of the world

like hunger, over-population, torture, crime-infested cities

disasters occur

personal tragedies—despair

life can also be unfair, unlucky, uninteresting, unnerving

for large parts of the day

or for years

Real people have bad moods
periods of depression
fall in love with someone who doesn't love them.

Real people very seldom are or become their dreams and fantasies of what they want to be.

Life has disappointments, unwelcome intrusions, boring tasks, unlucky breaks, accidents, prolonged bouts of bad weather, and physical ailments, to say nothing of oneself being seriously handicapped.

For many, long periods on welfare, unhappy marriages, ungrateful children.

Of course, there are joys and pleasures and excitements and orgasms. But these are occasional except when they dominate memories of good old days.

All other self-improvement books want you to pretend that you are the only reality. This book does not pretend. It acknowledges the pain of the real world, but it also says that:

   Optimism is easier than pessimism.

Wisdom, daydreaming, and risk-taking introduce you to options that you never felt possible.

DISCOVERING WHO WE ARE

Remember First…Failure Is an Event, NOT a Person.

**Sit Down in a Quiet Place
and Get in Touch with Yourself.**

WHO AM I?

Do you find yourself looking for yourself? What does that mean? I am not sure *I* know, but a lot of young people come to me and say they can't find themselves or that life, for them, has no meaning. They want to get it together, so they go on trips. Sometimes after these trips they come to me and confess, "I've never been so lonely and unhappy in my life." This is what I say: Life is not a meaning. It is an opportunity. Life is made up of a series of meaningful experiences that often last only a short time.

One of the most important survival tips for lonely people to know is this: Don't trust anyone who says that s/he is not trying to influence you. Be especially critical of people who claim they are fair, objective, perfectly honest and who start sentences with, "To tell the truth." Never, never trust anyone who says, "You can trust me."

Are you puzzled? Why should you be? I don't expect you to trust me. And besides, I only give advice that people find hard to follow. I have too much respect for the complexity of personality to expect that people can follow advice. Try these for size:

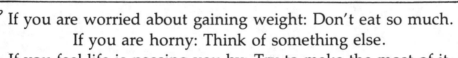
If you are worried about gaining weight: Don't eat so much.
If you are horny: Think of something else.
If you feel life is passing you by: Try to make the most of it.

I think that if people can, in fact, follow your advice, you are insulting them by offering it. The only advice worth giving is advice people cannot easily follow:

Not "advice" like
    Be Good
    Pay Attention
      which is never worthwhile, but 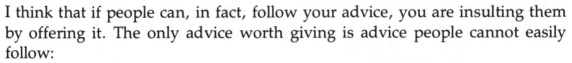 **WAIT!**

Let me make another point first. Behavior based on trust is often a way of avoiding responsibility. If you want to do something, do it as a risk, an unselfish act, an opportunity—but not because someone asks you to trust him/her. Take responsibility for what you do!

Say (to yourself): "I am telling you (a friend) my innermost secrets because I have a need to tell someone, and because I want to risk the possibility that you may betray me. If you do betray me I will be hurt and disappointed. If you prove to be a good friend I will be joyful." But don't say (or cry), "I told you my secrets because I trusted you." Or (the ultimate immaturity), "Now I can't trust anybody." Translation: *I will act as though everybody hates me.*

I tell people what I'm telling you now: Don't do anything on trust alone. You may continue to operate on trust but, if it doesn't work out, you will remember what I said and after more mistakes later you may be able to change your behavior. The price? Change may make you tense, uncomfortable and nervous. It's hard to shift gears. The reason people overeat is that eating relieves tension. If you reduce your intake you become very anxious. Having to tolerate the tension is the price you pay for weight reduction.

Sometimes, no matter how much you try, and despite your best intentions, you can't change the behavior you find unacceptable. This is because your personality needs that behavior; it is a defense against some worry or fear that is worse.

> A young man thinks he wants to stop stuttering but discovers that he doesn't really want to because he needs it so that people can feel sorry for him. No amount of speech therapy will help him until he can gain some confidence in himself.
>
> A mother overprotects her child because she has never felt secure as a mother and if anything happened to the child it would be "her fault." Telling her that she is being overprotective will fall on deaf ears until she works out the problem of her own insecurity.

The two examples given above illustrate conflicts that can require professional help from a trained social worker, psychologist, counselor or psychiatrist.

So what I am saying is that if you can't work out your problems by yourself or with the help of parents or friends, seek out professional guidance. But (warning) do not respond to your impulse to trust or not to trust the helper. Tell him/her what is on your mind but:

 — risk the helper's not helping
not understanding
not having the time or interest

 miss out on an opportunity

the helper will like you
will help you
will influence your life

Now I will give advice to people who can profit from advice that is awfully hard to follow.

If you are in a situation that is bad, try to improve or change it. If you can't, it may be because you are too young or too chicken or because the odds against you (as with some schools and families) are too heavy. In that case discover strategies of toleration and compromise but:

DON'T

PUNISH

YOURSELF

because of someone else's problem.

Pass the course you hate. Why punish yourself twice by having to take it over again?

● **Don't continue a relationship only because you don't want to hurt the other person's feelings. This is punishing yourself and the other person while giving you a false sense of being a nice person.**

● **Sometimes it is possible to change things and feel good about it. One group of students persisted in their demands for a birth-control clinic on campus (and won). Another group "forced" the introduction of sex education, another is still struggling for a more flexible curriculum.**

The point is that feeling rotten about yourself — whether expressed in terms of "the world is evil," "school is irrevelant," or "there is nothing to do"—is a cop-out. It is helpful to no one, even if the motivation for your view of the world seems to be sympathy for the poor or opposition to dictatorships. Sometimes you can't do much about the outside world except wait (painfully) until you are able to achieve a position of power and influence.

People who are messed up spend most of their time and energy hurting themselves and/or others. Their behavior tends to be involuntary, repetitive, and exploitative.

A kid into heavy drinking lies to friends and parents about how he is going to change. He maintains his habit by stealing and borrowing money, which he will never return. He hates himself because he is most hateful to people who care about him.

A girl spends most of her time thinking about all the people who hate her. All the people who are supposed to hate her don't even know she exists.

A boy finds school irrevelant, the world meaningless. He spends most of his time sleeping, not doing his school work, and quarreling with his brother and mother. He is so busy not doing things and fighting that he has no time for friends and pleasure. His current anger is that his parents do not want to reward him for his hostility by giving him a motorcycle (and some money besides) so he can travel around the country "finding himself."

A pretty girl is fed up with all the superficiality in life. She wants to be liked for her own sake. She dresses unattractively, doesn't wash much, and is more or less accepted as one of the boys—but she cannot understand why no boy wants to take her out (though quite a few wouldn't mind sleeping with her).

The meantime determines very largely what will happen in your future. Waiting until you get the courses you like ("and then I'll study") often means you won't reach that point. Trying to improve a marriage by having children usually ends up making matters much worse. (Who was it who said, "The road to hell is paved with good intentions"?)

It is not difficult to know when you are doing the wrong thing. (You really have to be in a bad way not to know—like a criminal who feels there is nothing wrong with what he does except if he gets caught.)

The chances are that if you are not doing what is right for you, symptoms, such as these, will appear:

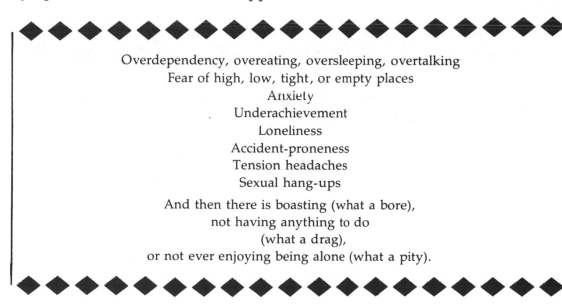

Overdependency, overeating, oversleeping, overtalking
Fear of high, low, tight, or empty places
Anxiety
Underachievement
Loneliness
Accident-proneness
Tension headaches
Sexual hang-ups

And then there is boasting (what a bore),
not having anything to do
(what a drag),
or not ever enjoying being alone (what a pity).

We all get depressed at times. Sometimes feeling down in the dumps lasts a long time. Professional help may be needed to get out of it, but more often than not an opportune phone call will put you in good spirits. Let me, however, suggest a strategy that can occasionally be used to speed up getting back into the swing of things. You are depressed, upset, moody, irritable, bitchy, or whatever. Look up a new word in a dictionary, glance at an encyclopedia, almanac, or one of the news weeklies. Learning something new is very stimulating. The next step is calling someone and having a long conversation, or going out for a walk or run (or standing on your head). Before you know it, the down cycle is broken. The more you do, the better you feel. This is especially true of people who spend a lot of time thinking about what they'd like to do or all the things they feel guilty about (or people who are chronic worriers). Remember, too, that even if you have a lot of self-awareness it is of little practical value unless you can act on it.

THE 10 MOST UNNECESSARY FEARS

(in order of unreasonable fearsomeness)

1 FEAR OF THE OPPOSITE SEX
2 FEAR OF THE SAME SEX
3 FEAR THAT YOU MIGHT BE A HOMOSEXUAL
4 FEAR THAT NO ONE WILL WANT TO HAVE SEX WITH YOU
5 FEAR OF INTIMACY
6 FEAR THAT YOU WON'T MEASURE UP TO SOMEONE ELSE'S STANDARDS
7 FEAR OF RISKING NEW EXPERIENCES
8 FEAR THAT IF YOU ARE NICE TO PEOPLE THEY WILL TAKE ADVANTAGE OF YOU
9 FEAR THAT LIFE WILL PASS YOU BY
10 FEAR THAT ALL THERE IS TO LIFE IS WHAT YOU'VE EXPERIENCED ALREADY

 # WARNING

Try not to be desperate about anything you do. Cool it, be patient. If necessary, pretend you have savoir faire (if you don't know what it means, look it up). Live in the present. Stop trying to please the people you don't care about.

If, after reading this book, you still have one or more of the above ten fears, you have not read it carefully or taken it seriously enough. So read it again. Discuss it with a friend. And if you still have at least one of those fears, get help.

If you don't know what to say, listen to what other people are saying. You might have something to say (after all).

You don't have to be a big psychologist to appreciate that the process of not learning is exhausting. Students who don't learn much at school are tired at the end of the day. If you want energy during after-school activities, learn — for your own protection.

If you want to know whether you were oversleeping (let's say for 12 hours or more) because you physically needed it or because you were psychologically afraid to face the next day, you can *always* judge it by whether, after oversleeping, you were refreshed or woke up tired.

If you have a persistent, uncomfortable dream or nightmare, your unconscious is giving you a message that you have an unresolved conflict. If you resolve the conflict you will no longer have the repetitive dream.

Rational guilt can be distinguished from irrational guilt by how you handle it. Genuine guilt organizes you. It helps you avoid making the same mistake again and has a tendency to make you feel better about yourself. Irrational guilt encourages a tendency for self-pity or a wish for punishment so you can feel free to do *it* again. Rational guilt (something you should feel after doing something wrong) is healthy. Irrational guilt (something you feel despite the fact that you did nothing wrong—the worst kind being when you feel guilty about thoughts and fantasies) always makes you feel bad about yourself, and the energy keeps that guilt alive and unwell.

What counts is not what a person says so much as what he does. Sometimes behavior such as forgetfulness or passivity communicates more hostility than a big verbal argument. "I love you" is worth only as much as how it is expressed in day-to-day behavior...in acts of kindness.

There is no way of avoiding tension, upsets, and frustrations, but when these become the dominant forces in life, then life becomes one big hassle, whether it is expressed in terms of "life has no meaning" or "everybody hates me." People who are striving to find meaning in a mature way are people whose lives are made up of meaningful choices. They always have more to do than there is time for. They have alternatives. They take risks. They can enjoy being alone at times. They know that when it is more important to them to meet the needs of the other person than to satisfy their own, they are in love.

If you don't feel that your life has just been described, work to make it psychologically healthy.

It's hard work. Life is hard work. If you have a genuine problem, the

7

shift from the conflict to a state of health is rarely easy or automatic. The shift (the work of resolving the conflict) usually requires boring, mechanical, and tension-producing efforts.

 If your hang-up is studying and it is important *for you* to do your work—you will seldom reach a point when you really feel like doing it. You must do it despite your feeling of not wanting to. Set yourself realistic goals. "I'll study for 30 minutes, then I'll watch TV for 30 minutes, then I'll study for 40 minutes and then I'll eat a snack," etc. "I'm going to study for four hours straight" usually ends up in not studying at all.

If your hang-up is being afraid of girls/boys there is no way you are going to feel comfortable with them without having a lot of experience of being comfortable with yourself first, being comfortable with members of your own sex second, and then slowly working through your conflicts with the opposite sex. Upon reaching the third stage you can't help but *feel* uncomfortable and awkward on your first dates. And unless you *are* willing to risk rejection, you won't even reach the stage of your first date. What is not often understood is that *risking rejection is also risking acceptance.*

How you feel about something is no substitute for the hard, anxiety-producing and, often, mechanical work required for problem-solving. Spontaneity develops after the conflict is resolved; it is seldom the medium for conflict-resolution.

Are you looking for yourself or the meaning in life? I hope so, because finding the meaning of life is a lifelong struggle that consists of trying to put together meaningful experiences. Getting it together is life itself.

"UNEXPECTED TRAVEL SUGGESTIONS ARE DANCING LESSONS FROM GOD."
— Kurt Vonnegut

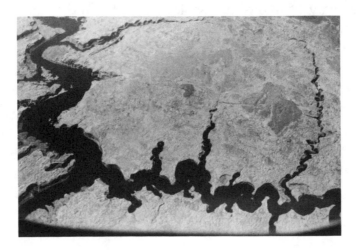

WHAT IS NORMAL?

Normal is a word. But not a normal word. It is a *loaded* word. And like other loaded words, it is sometimes used as a weapon to keep you in line.

For example, people often use "normal" as a label to describe people and situations they consider to be "safe" or nonthreatening. Likewise, people often call "abnormal" the people and things they don't like, don't agree with, or that are just "different."

Some people feel that you are normal when you are able to adjust to and accept the status quo and other written and unwritten "rules" handed down by the Establishment (as those in positions of power are sometimes called). That is, normal behavior is frequently thought to be behavior that *conforms* to society's jumble of taboos, fears, customs, rules, and laws. If what you are doing does not conform to what parents, friends and teachers expect, they say you are not dealing with "real" things and that this isn't normal. They may be right, but,

when you get down to it
only you
can decide
what is true
for you

reality
can change as
you grow

If *normal* means conformity to rules and regulations (which change from culture to culture and from time to time), then dissenters, reformers, and creative people will be branded as *abnormal*.

Similarly, we must be wary of accepting the majority's view as the norm. For example, prejudice against minority groups, such as blacks, Mexican-Americans, Puerto Ricans, Indians, and Jews is common in America. But is it normal to be prejudiced against some people just because many, or most, members of your own group are prejudiced against these "outsiders"? Is it normal to follow the latest fashions or fads because "stars" are doing it or because the mass media tell us what is "in" and "out"?

Rather than worry about what is normal, we might think about *what is not abnormal.*

For one thing, it is not abnormal to refuse to accept and adjust to all existing conditions. Martin Luther King, for example, refused to go along with segregationist laws and customs. By intelligent, well-planned protest and opposition, he was able to trigger off important changes (including the 1964 Civil Rights Act). Likewise, it is not abnormal for us to crusade against common evils like pollution, slums, corruption in business and government or the exploitation of one person by another.

Conformity for its own sake is not a measure of normality.

Super-conformists or super-nonconformists, at best, tend to lead boring lives.

Nonconformity as an act of conscience can be a courageous and enriching force in a person's life, as demonstrated by the thousands of young men who refused to be drafted for the war in Vietnam. In a sense, these resisters can be accused of premature morality.

A SCALE FOR MEASURING ADJUSTMENT AND MALADJUSTMENT

Perhaps, when discussing purely personal behavior, it would be better to abandon the notion of normality altogether. Rather than casually brand someone as "normal" or "abnormal" we might think in terms of an "adjustment—maladjustment" scale, as follows.

You have:

● **Excellent adjustment** if you enjoy life, have friends, work close to your maximum abilities, have a sound relationship with your family, make satisfying use of your leisure time, and if you can generally cope with your problems.

● **Good adjustment** if your behavior is excellent in most areas of everyday life and personality development, but is less than excellent in a few areas.

● **Adequate adjustment** if you get along reasonably well and have no problems so serious that they overwhelm you. You have ups and downs, but you also have friends and enjoyable interests.

● **Poor adjustment** if you have at least one serious problem (see the following list of six) but still do well in at least one area, such as schoolwork or relationships with friends.

● **Very poor adjustment** if you have one or more problems so severe as to be disabling, or with symptoms that threaten future personality development. Poorly adjusted young people often appear to be on the road to addictions, to mental illness or delinquency, or give the impression of being grossly inadequate.

SIX
SIGNS OF VERY POOR ADJUSTMENT

You have made a poor or very poor adjustment to life if you show at least one of the following signs:

1 An inability to learn at a level close to what your intelligence would call for. (And if this gap is not caused by brain damage or other health problems; or by language barriers resulting from recent immigration; or by a move from an area with a backward educational system; or by temporary conditions, such as grief over the breaking up of an important relationship.)
2 An inability to build and maintain satisfactory relationships with other people, especially people in the same age group. (This sign is important only if it lasts for a long time.)
3 Continued inappropriate or immature behavior in everyday circumstances. Such behavior might include silliness, bizarre mannerisms, or frequent aggressive outbursts, as well as apathy as a common response to frustration.
4 A persistent mood of unhappiness or depression. This does not refer to a temporary reaction of shock triggered by the death of a loved one, for instance. And it does not apply to occasional anxiety, tension, and unhappiness, which are all part of *normal* growth and development.
5 Fears or physical symptoms (such as stuttering, tics, pains, and phobias) that develop in response to personal and school problems.
6 Compulsive behavior. Almost everyone has a bad habit or two, but sometimes behaviors get far enough beyond your control (such as overeating or super-orderliness) that they become the focus of a lot of anxiety.

Remember: The poorly adjusted person doesn't necessarily show all these symptoms. Also, even the most maladjusted person may sometimes have areas of adequacy, or even demonstrate exceptional talents and accomplishments. Jimi Hendrix and Jim Morrison, for instance, were tremendous musicians but evidently couldn't cope with the rest of life.

FANTASY, REALITY, & NORMALITY

All of us have a *fantasy life.*

This is made up of dreams, imaginings, wishes, impulses, and the like, which often originate in the unconscious. At the deeper levels of the mind, these elements represent the raw, primitive, amoral forces in the personality. Thus, from time to time, we become aware of impulses or desires that may seem murderous, suicidal, sensuous, sadistic, romantic, weird, sexual, heroic, or incestuous.

If we feel guilty or frightened by these ideas, they are likely to occur again and again. *Guilt provides the energy for the compulsive (involuntary) repetition of images that are unacceptable or even repulsive to us.* This is a very important idea, and we repeat it elsewhere in this book.

The point to keep in mind is that fantasizing and daydreaming are entirely normal. They are a healthy and, indeed, a necessary part of life. For example, we may enjoy fantasies of a sexual nature, and we may choose to repeat them again and again, even though we know that we cannot carry them out. In one sense, fantasy is part of the reality of preparing for life as an adult. In fact, in all of us, *fantasy is part of the reality of life.*

Thus, you should reject the fear that any kinds of thoughts can in themselves be abnormal or can drive you crazy.

However, it is clear that fantasy can also become an escape, a cop-out, a way of avoiding life. Guilt-ridden, uncontrolled fantasizing is a symptom of internal conflicts, such as feelings of inferiority.

IS SOCIETY ABNORMAL?

As R. D. Laing has pointed out, in the last 50 years, "normal" people have killed more than 100 million of their fellow normal people.

No one can make you feel inferior without your consent.

4 QUESTIONS:

The next time you think of anyone, including yourself, in terms of normal and abnormal, consider the following questions:

1 Is the use of the concept of normality the real issue—or is it really a means of avoiding the issue?
2 Is it being used as an attack against a nonconformist who may be a creative, healthy person with ideas that you don't like?
3 Is it being used on the basis of an unexamined assumption that anything the majority does, thinks, or likes is thereby good—and "normal"?
4 Is it being used as a way of debasing or hating yourself?

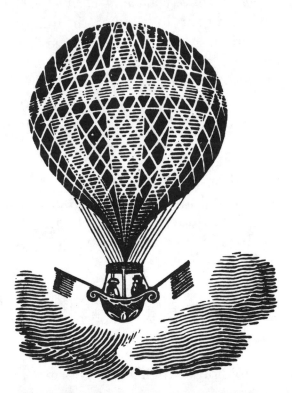

☞ HAVE YOU EVER HEARD OF ANYONE WHO ENJOYS LIFE WHO DOESN'T ALSO ENJOY DAYDREAMING?

FOR PEOPLE
WHO SUFFER FROM BEING
A MINORITY

A minority is someone who feels or is different from most people or who feels abused because of circumstances s/he has no control over.

In a sense, women are a majority who are a minority.

In a way, just about everyone is a minority—but that fact doesn't help people who are discriminated against. Neither does that fact do much good for people who are victims of circumstances even though there may be a rational reason for their situation (as with children who are upset and confused after their parents separate).

Another example: There are some Jews who don't like the fact that they are Jewish and they become like the anti-Semites. They identify with the aggressor. That is, they operate—perhaps unconsciously—as though the accusations by the bigots were generally true.

(It just goes to show that, no matter who you are, if you think in stereotypes it's very easy to ''prove'' any point you want.)

On the other hand, Jews who accept their Jewishness—whether because of parents, Jewish culture, or identification with Israel—generally feel better about themselves and have a fine sense of self-acceptance.

What we are getting at is that the best way to cope with being a minority is to accept, rather than fight, your background. This goes for handicapped people too. People who are preoccupied with their handicap are a burden onto themselves and others. What happens then is that the poor self-image and depression become even more of a burden than the disability itself.

Any experience can be turned to your advantage. The way to do this is to get involved and find out what it means.

So . . .

If you're black, learn about the history of the black experience.

If you're a woman, know your rights.

If you're Jewish, think about the good points of Jewish pride and Jewish history.

If you're deaf, accept that *other* deaf people are as good as people who aren't deaf.

If you're gay, discover that you're a person first and foremost.

Once you know these things, *then* you are able to decide whether to be or not to be an activist.

15

FOR PEOPLE
WHO HAVE A DISABILITY

If you are not yourself "handicapped" in some way, you very probably know someone, a relative or friend, who is. According to the American Coalition of Citizens with Disabilities, about 36 million Americans today—roughly one in six—suffer from serious physical, mental, or emotional impairments.

Being handicapped is not easy. It involves all kinds of difficulties—social, emotional, sexual, and, of course, economic. Part of the problem lies in the fact that *people who have a disability are often excluded from the mainstream of life by the rest of us.*

As a psychologist who has worked for more than a quarter of a century with the problems of handicapped people, I have some "advice" to offer. First, to people who do not suffer from any special disabilities: Make an effort to be a friend to a person who is handicapped. Not out of pity, but out of empathy and compassion—as an aspect of being a decent human being. Form your friendship by seeking out a common interest, or by helping the person take an interest in an area you find rewarding. Once a real relationship has been established, don't treat the person with exaggerated "delicacy" or "sensitivity." Such an attitude is likely to do far more harm than good. In particular, don't hesitate to convey frankly what pleases and displeases you. For example, you may find that your new friend is "overdoing it," or misinterpreting your friendly interest for love. If this is so, the sooner and more decisively you straighten things out, the better.

Here is another important point:
It's all right to start out feeling uncomfortable. Very few people can be fully comfortable at first in the company of someone who is, let's say, blind, deaf, or cerebral-palsied. By acknowledging your discomfort, you don't have to move quickly to pity, shame, guilt, rejection, or withdrawal. Talk about your discomfort, and then your friend may be able to explain, directly or indirectly, how to deal with it.

Now a few "messages" to a person who has a disability:

1. No one can make you feel inferior without your consent.
2. If you have interests, someone will be interested in you.
3. If you are chronically bored, you will be boring to be with.
4. If you have nothing to do, don't do it with anyone else around.
5. (and most important) Our society does not give you "points" for being handicapped. You need to work hard to make friends and to prove to everybody—

*that you are a person first.
*that your handicap is secondary to everything that is important to you.

FOR PEOPLE
WHO DON'T THINK THEY
ARE ATTRACTIVE

People who are self-accepting are sexually attractive to *some* other people—period. It doesn't matter what the cosmetic and toothpaste industries have to say about it.

It's not that short, fat, or "unattractive" people can't "find" a mate; it's that people who hate themselves and express it in being (not looking) unattractive, shortsighted, or fatuous tend to repel, rather than attract, others.

Believing that certain perfumes, hair tonics, vaginal sprays, or selective techniques or positions will make you attractive will get you nowhere. *Being* a good person is what is attractive to other people. You'd be surprised; more and more people these days are into being authentic. We are in a "let's stop playing games" era.

THERE IS SOMEBODY FOR EVERYBODY

FOR PEOPLE
WHO ARE ESPECIALLY
BRIGHT OR SENSITIVE

If you want to develop your mental health, your self-esteem, your intelligence, your skills, you will have to put up with a lot of abuse and snubbing from people who are less ambitious. However, once you have established your own identity and have your own circle of friends, this won't matter at all.

By the way, people who are exceptionally sensitive and intelligent often go to great pains to hide these qualities. People get on to you anyway, though, and they will resent what they sense is a kind of reverse snobbery.

If you don't acknowledge high-level intellectual qualities in yourself, you are cheating yourself. You tend to play down your abilities when talking with people; thus you might miss out on someone who is interested in you, rather than afraid of you.

When you repress an important part of your personality, you begin to act phoney. Putting up this artificial front causes a lot of strain and diverts energy that you might use more profitably elsewhere.

Besides, it's really a drag for people who sense your tension and don't know how to relate to you. In our sexist culture, this pitfall is especially true for women.

None of this means you should be a "typical" arrogant intellectual. (Arrogance is basically an irrational form of defense that blocks possibilities for intimacy.)

You just have to find some way to be a self-expressing person.

FOR PEOPLE WHO HAVE BEEN INSULTED

The fear of being humiliated is one of the biggest blocks to being the way you want to be.

A lot of people are more afraid of being shamed and ridiculed than they are of being beaten up.

Some pointers:

● Don't take seriously the opinions of people you don't respect.

● Some people enjoy provoking and taunting others into getting flustered. They usually do it when they have an audience.

One very effective way of handling this form of abuse is — believe it or not — to ignore it. Your antagonist will generally try to get a rise out of you for a while, until he starts to look silly in front of his audience because you aren't responding.

Sometimes playing along a little with the attack will neutralize it. If someone calls you stupid, maybe you can agree, "Yup. I'm so stupid, you wouldn't believe how stupid I am." Then, go on with your business and don't dwell on or drag out the exchange. By agreeing in an exaggerated — but controlled — way, you have blocked your opponent. At any rate, whatever your reply, it should be conscious and calculated.

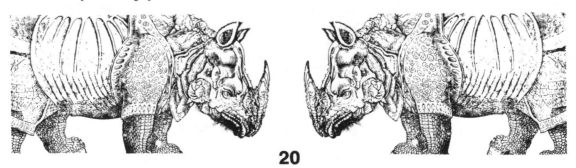

● Try to figure out the reason for the insult. For example, possibly you were a little too thin-skinned and the "insult" was basically good-natured ribbing, or well-deserved and well-intended criticism that might be helpful for you to accept.

Of course, some snipers are habitually nasty. The cutting remark is perfectly timed to deflate your ego. Even if the criticism is true, ask yourself how much it really means. Some people inflate their overly insecure egos by deflating others: Why should other people be hung up in your "faults" or problems? Possibly because you remind them of things they are worried about in themselves.

● What do you do about this classic insult: "You'll never amount to anything"?
The best answer: "I know it, and that's what worries me about myself."
They say: "So why don't you *do* something about it?"
You answer: "Like you often say, it's easier said than done."
If that doesn't end it, say that you need to be alone for a while.

The point is not that you agree that you won't amount to anything, but that you are using a strategy to shut off a fruitless argument.

● If an insult comes from someone you don't know very well, the hell with it. If it comes from a good friend, a relative, or someone you love, don't let it bother you.

Be concerned only if their insults are habitual. Then figure out: What are you going to do about it?

FOR PEOPLE
WHO DEMAND EVERYTHING
— OR NOTHING

All-or-none type people typically want everything—or nothing at all. If their room can't be completely organized and tidy, they leave it a complete mess. If they can't be in complete control of a relationship, they break it up. If they can't do a job all in one session, they give up. If they don't think they can get the Gold Medal, they don't enter the contest.

They are basically unrealistic people, easily intimidated by phrases like: "If a job is worth doing, it's worth doing right." That's a nice idea, as long as you don't use it to block yourself from doing anything at all.

If perfectionism is a hang-up of yours, here's a tip:

   LOWER YOUR STANDARDS
SO YOU CAN INCREASE
YOUR PERFORMANCE.

21

Some people feel they are not qualified to help anyone else because they are not together enough themselves. Sure, you should try to get it together. That's life. But part of getting it together is realizing that the stronger should help the weaker.

If you want self-confidence, try taking some responsibility for someone else's welfare. For example, do volunteer work at your local crisis center or free clinic. Or find outlets in which you can share yourself with children.

Becoming an active carer may not solve all your problems, but —if you're lucky—you'll find that they aren't nearly as overwhelming as they used to be. When people are relying on *you* to get something done that really needs doing, you shouldn't have time to be overly hung up on your personal problems.

FOR PEOPLE
WHO SMOKE, SMOKE, SMOKE
. . . SMOKE THAT CIGARETTE

Some people are so insecure about their image that they'll try anything that might give them a little boost of confidence.

Kids who have recently taken up cigarettes almost always "enjoy" smoking when others are around to see them. Smoking *looks* tough, or cool, or adult, or whatever. And, best of all, adults don't like it when teenagers smoke.

It's so dumb. Is the small bit of pleasure you get from tobacco worth risking addiction? Addiction sneaks up on you and you don't even know you're hooked—until one day you run out of cigarettes and you go crazy trying to get some. Some teenagers suffer from the screwy idea that being addicted to cigarettes somehow makes them more grown up. Actually, after a while it is really degrading to be a slave to nicotine. Blah . . .

Notice that the people in the cigarette ads are almost always young, attractive, hip, suave, carefree, sexy, successful, manly, and so on. These ads are aimed at *kids*. Once a person gets past age 20 or so s/he won't ordinarily start smoking, no matter *what*.

"WARNING: THE SURGEON GENERAL HAS DETERMINED THAT CIGARETTE SMOKING IS DANGEROUS TO YOUR HEALTH."

FOR PEOPLE
WHO ARE WORRYWARTS

WORRYING IS GOOD FOR YOU
SOMETIMES.

I get fed up with people who tell me not to worry, especially doctors who use it as an excuse not to tell me what I am entitled to know, and self-centered busybodies and know-nothings who think that my worries don't amount to much because only their own worries are the *real ones*.

People like this are always telling me:

You have nothing to worry about.

You call that something to worry about?

That should be your worst worry.

So, what's the worry?

Worrying doesn't help.

It doesn't pay to worry.

Worrying isn't good for you.

Don't worry. It'll all work out in the end.

Is that all you've got to worry about?

My dear, let me tell you about real worries.

Sometimes I use a lot of relatively unimportant worries to block out temporarily big, important worries that I can't do anything about. It's very helpful to me to do that—even though intellectually I realize that it would be better to do something constructive.

But sometimes I don't have the peace of mind or the will or the energy and that's all right too.

And sometimes worrying is the background or even the inspiration for a creative idea that I can write down, even after a restless night.

If one really good thought or plan emerges, it would be worth it after all.

The best worrying leads to some action and resolution. But it's very difficult to turn off real worries (as I think about it, all worries are real). Worrying becomes destructive when it interferes with everything else you want to do, when it's used as a weapon against other people, and when it's repressed and turns into symptoms.

I worry a lot because I have a lot to worry about. I don't want a worrywart telling me not to worry. I worry a lot and I get a lot done too.

LIVING FULLY

If you've had fun-tell everyone

"Never, never, for the sake of peace
and quiet deny your own experience."

new experiences

Sometimes I think our world is full of "experts" who claim to have solutions for everybody else's problems. With all the people offering us happiness by reading certain books, eating certain foods, believing certain prophets, or watching certain stars, it's little wonder that life remains full of uncertainties. I often wonder if human beings aren't so mixed up that they must put a lot of energy into getting themselves together. The less together they are the more of their time is spent unproductively being angry. They are too angry for love or new experiences.

Life is funny sometimes. If you want something done, you ask a busy person to do it. If you need support, don't ask for it from people who can't support themselves.

People who hate themselves hate a lot of people in the process. It took me a long time to discover this. I remember a day of terrific insight—sitting around a pool rapping with a friend. What a time we had. We spent four hours talking about all the people we hated until it dawned on us: All the people we hated were having a good time swimming and loving while we were talking about them. What a waste of time!

Psychology opens up the world—our dreams, our fantasies, our wishes, and our experiences help us in the never-ending process of defining ourselves. If our definition excludes fantasies or the awareness of the infinite number of possible events and opportunities, our life is boring and tiring. If our life is dominated by self-doubts, fears, or compulsions, we become too busy protecting, hiding, or kidding ourselves to do our own thing. The

If you are not controversial, you have nothing to offer.

things we do tend to be self-destructive or exploitative. And if people also have to worry about being poor or being victims of discrimination, it really is rough.

Life is complicated. But getting your life together does not mean that you can't enjoy contradictions, or unrelated and isolated experiences. Sometimes I meet someone for a brief moment and it's love at first sight, knowing full well I'll never see that person again. Sometimes I think about being a poet—and even write a lot of poems, knowing that I may not be a poet. I sense that poets write poetry and are serious and I write poetry and I am not sure I'm serious.

I don't know much about photography, but the idea fascinated me and I set out to express the fascination by taking fascinating pictures. The result: a new experience. Now I take photographs for pleasure. But does it mean that I am not a photographer because no one will buy my pictures or will give me a diploma?

I never thought I could write. But after a "civil rights" Mississippi interlude some years ago I wrote about it. Here is an excerpt:

> I have been around enough psychologists to know that most of us have three main (secret) ambitions in life. The first is to write a novel; the second is to be a hero; and the third is to be able to exchange, at will, one set of neurotic symptoms for another. Any psychologist who would like to enjoy an instantaneous illusion of realizing all three ambitions should spend a civil rights summer in Mississippi.
>
> Upon arrival in Jackson, you feel like a hero (albeit in search of an heroic situation) and on your way to the Delta, your mind is pregnant with your novel. (I remember the first sentences of my "autobiographical" novel. I thought about writing something that psychologists would enjoy, something that would lend itself to "interpretation" and would readily be misunderstood.) Within twenty-four hours (unfortunately and whether you like it or not), whatever symptoms you start out with are traded in for paranoia.

I got a lot of praise for the thing I wrote. I'm not sure why—but suddenly I write. Maybe I am not a writer, but who cares?

I remember surviving my high school days by daydreaming a lot. It was the only relief I had from hating everything. (I was really messed up when I was a kid.) But, you know, I feel younger now than I did in those days. I do a lot of things and I am very seldom tired—it's weird in a way. In those days I hated:

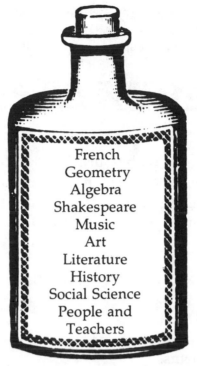

French
Geometry
Algebra
Shakespeare
Music
Art
Literature
History
Social Science
People and
Teachers

I daydreamed and read a lot of books that had sad endings.

Later, much later, when I was in France, I was angry that I didn't know French. Later, even later than I care to admit, I was tricked into seeing a Shakespearean play and I loved it. A new experience!

Now, whenever I can, I trick people into having new experiences. When I was teaching high school I assigned new experiences. Get a load of this assignment:

 You are required, in order to pass this course, to have several new experiences (sheer blackmail).

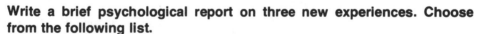 **Write a brief psychological report on three new experiences. Choose from the following list.**

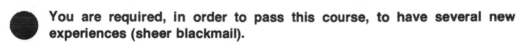

1　Read (not just look at) *Playboy* or *Playgirl.*
2　If you are a conservative, read from cover to cover *The New Republic.*
3　If you are a liberal, read from cover to cover the *National Review.*
4　If the only time you've ever been to an art museum is when the school dragged you along—visit a large art museum and spend your time trying to figure out why people visit art museums voluntarily. Even go so far as asking a stranger who seems to be enjoying the experience.
5　Go to a ballet.
6　Listen to an entire opera like *Aida.*
7　Get the Sunday edition of *The New York Times* and spend hours finding out why it is America's most prestigious newspaper.

8 If your everyday personality is grumpy, spend a whole day being nice to people.

9 If you have the philosophy that people should love you for what you are and not how you dress or act—try acting and dressing conventionally for a week and note carefully the responses you get from people you assumed shouldn't care.

Got the message?

Whatever you decide to do with your life—decide on the basis of a wide range of alternatives. New experiences help you make your choice. Don't decide in advance about all the things you hate and will always hate.

Look at all the new things you can try if you feel stuck:

1. Keep a diary.
2. Remember dreams.
3. Learn a new word each day.
4. Photograph trees.
5. Write one poem.
6. Write two poems.
7. Fly a kite.
8. Say hello to a person you think you should hate.
9. Decide on a country to visit in Europe. Read all about it first and
   then figure out how you are going to get there.
10. Read a short book like *Billy Budd*. Try to figure out why it is still popular.
11. Write me a letter.
12. Write a letter to someone you owe a letter to.
13. Go see a foreign film.
14. See a Chaplin film.
15. Figure out why some people think Andy Warhol was a genius and some people think he was cracked.
16. Imagine yourself in love with someone. Dream or write about it.
17. Discover a beautiful path for a long walk.
18. Try meditation.
19. Practice Yoga.

HERE ARE SOME THINGS I LOVE IN LIFE:*

The Declaration of Independence
Marc Chagall
Chocolate cake
Some students
The Sunday edition of *The New York Times*
Money that's for spending, and not saving in the bank for
      my old age or my wife's old age or my son to inherit
My wife (who is Danish)
T. S. Eliot
The New York City Ballet
Mozart
My home
What used to be the Beatles
Syracuse (the University, not the climate)
San Francisco, but Jerusalem even more
Israel in general
London in particular
A bunch of people who remain unnamed
The Museum of Modern Art in New York City
Chicago when the wind doesn't blow
A weekend in Savannah, Georgia

*And see how I've revised my list by the time I reach the end of the book.

Remember when the air was clean and sex was dirty?

People often ask me at parties if I read minds, I now answer, "Yes. I do."

MAKE UP YOUR LIST
OF SOME THINGS
YOU LOVE IN LIFE.

"There is absolutely no inevitability as long as there is a willingness to contemplate what is happening."
— Marshall McLuhan

WHEN YOU ARE BORED, YOU ARE BORING TO BE WITH

Everyone is bored, upset, or depressed now and then. That's of no particular significance. It's only when boredom or depression becomes a style of life that you have to get off your dead end.

There is nothing more uninteresting than a bunch of people standing around talking about how bored they are—which often ends up with them agreeing to go out and pick up somebody. Maybe one day you'll get the chance to see the film *Marty*, which immortalized what a drag the pick-up trip really is.

 Here is a list of the most boring things you can do:

1. Run yourself down. Tell yourself and others how worthless and rotten you are.
2. Similarly, when people ask you how you feel, tell them the details of your rottenness.
3. Tell people you're horney.
4. Boast about things that everybody knows you haven't done.
5. Watch more than an hour and a half of TV a day. Have you noticed? The more you watch, the more bored you get?
6. Masturbate not because you enjoy it, but because you have nothing else to do. Have you discovered that if you feel guilty, you hardly enjoy it at all?
7. Talk about only one subject (sports, girls, boys, etc.). It's OK to have one main interest, but if that's all you talk about, people won't listen.

31

8. Come across as Pollyannish (oh, everything is wonderful!); or cynical and sarcastic.
9. Relentlessly tell people you're tired.
10. Talk too much. It's not as boring to talk too little—as long as you participate by listening.
11. Complain a lot (ugh!).
12. Be paranoid and suspicious of everyone's motives. You're always thinking: "What do you want to know for, anyway?"
13. Relate to people without ever risking being intimate (which also means risking rejection).
14. Be super-dependent on what other people think of you. They get the message that they can't talk frankly with you.
15. Begin your approach to people by saying, "I don't want to trouble you—bore you—take up too much of your time. . ." It's fake humility.
16. Not be open to new experiences.
17. Be a super-miser. You don't want to do the most interesting things because "you can't afford it." It will be forever before you can afford it.
18. Persistently analyze the motives of everyone's behavior.
19. Be a gossip. (Super boring.)
20. Nearly always wait to be asked; hardly ever ask.
21. Almost always be serious and humorless; or almost never be serious, and kid around all the time.
22. Relieve tension *mainly* with drugs or alcohol.
23. Almost never tolerate being alone at times.
24. Lead an unexamined life.
25. Spoil other people's stories (because you've said, thought, heard it before).
26. Trust no one; or trust everybody.
27. Announce how self-sacrificing you are and
28. What ungrateful slobs the rest are.
29. Complain that there's nothing to do, or talk endlessly of future plans that usually don't pan out . . .

If you're bored
turn to page 112 and look at
a fabulous picture.

Never take to heart the opinions of people you don't respect.

18 THINGS TO DO BY YOURSELF

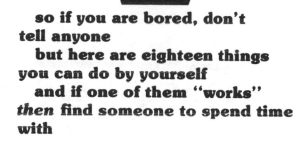

so if you are bored, don't
tell anyone
but here are eighteen things
you can do by yourself
and if one of them "works"
then find someone to spend time
with

1. Write a letter to someone who would be surprised to hear from you.
2. Give yourself a massage.
3. Write a Haiku (a 17-syllable poem arranged in three lines of 5, 7, and 5 syllables).
4. Go to a park, museum, or a play—something you would *never* think of doing by yourself.
5. In a dictionary find five words that you've heard of but don't know the meaning of—study them until you do.
6. Munch a carrot very slowly.
7. Watch a program on TV that you wouldn't ordinarily watch—like a documentary on P. B. S.
8. Go see a serious—not a frivolous—movie.
9. Purchase a magazine that you wouldn't ordinarily read—like *Sassy,*

New Republic, the *Humanist, Utne Reader, Rolling Stone, Teen,* or *Seventeen* and read at least two articles in it.

10. Discover the radio. Don't watch TV a whole day (a whole week would be better). Find out what radio has to offer *aside from* your favorite music.

11. Be your own psycho-drama. Act out a *scene* for at least 20 minutes that you would like to play in real life. Be very animated and enthusiastic.

12. Bake bread or cookies from scratch.

13. Take a warm bath.

14. Write down all the things you really like to do. Don't stop until you've written down at least a number equivalent to your age. If you are 20 years old you *should* be able to write 20 things you really enjoy—and add at least one to the list every year. Then, without giving it much thought, *do* one of the things on your list.

15. Go shopping and buy something for yourself—spend a little more than you can afford.

16. Daydream without feeling guilty.

17. Fix or build something.

18. If nothing else works, try exercise.

The Most Boring Conversation

Any of these responses to the question:
"What would you like to do?"

I don't know.
It doesn't make any difference to me.
What do *you* want to do?
There is nothing *to do.*

If you have nothing to do...
don't do it 👉 here

Do you have ants in your plants?

People I like:

1. Have a sense of humor
2. Have a passionate interest in some things
3. Have high energy levels
4. Are tolerant of my changing moods
5. Know how to listen
6. Are creative
7. Enjoy touching
8. Are enthusiastic
9. Exude self-confidence
10. Appreciate my successes—are sympathetic when I fail
11. Appreciate when we can be together—don't fuss when we are not
12. Have a keen sense of justice and injustice
13. Are sensitive to the needs of others
14. Can take risks
15. Have an air of mystery about them
16. Are not sure of everything
17. Are optimistic
18. Don't make fun of people
19. Can offer love unselfishly
20. Are people in whose presence I like myself more

NEW TEACHERS
SINCE THE LAST TIME
I MET YOU

When the mind is ready
a Teacher appears

Wisdom is learning what to overlook.

William James

Sometimes the best we can do is to risk giving without anticipation of return.

John S. Rice

Every death has a life of its own.

Marian Leavitt

Enlightenment doesn't care how you get there.

Thaddeus Golas

The model for loving our neighbors is always based on the way we love ourselves.

Eugene Kennedy

Love is letting go of fear.

Gerald G. Jampolsky

The power of God is the worship God inspires. What power is greater than the power that simply says: "I love you and for that reason I want you to be the best you can be"?

Rabbi Chaim Stern

Prayer invites God to let His presence suffuse our spirits, to let His will prevail in our lives. Prayer cannot bring water to parched fields, or mend a broken bridge, or rebuild a ruined city; but prayer can water an arid soul, mend a broken heart, and rebuild a weakened will.

Reform Prayer Book

Honesty is not necessarily self-disclosure. It is saying what you mean.

Sylvia Hacker

For the principle of love is not merely affection for each other. It connotes tolerance, helpfulness, willingness to share each other's resources, and, above all, rendering unto others the respect and the consideration that equals deserve from one another.

David Lawrence

Contentment
is not
the fulfillment
of what you
want
but the
realization
of how much
you already
have

Anon.

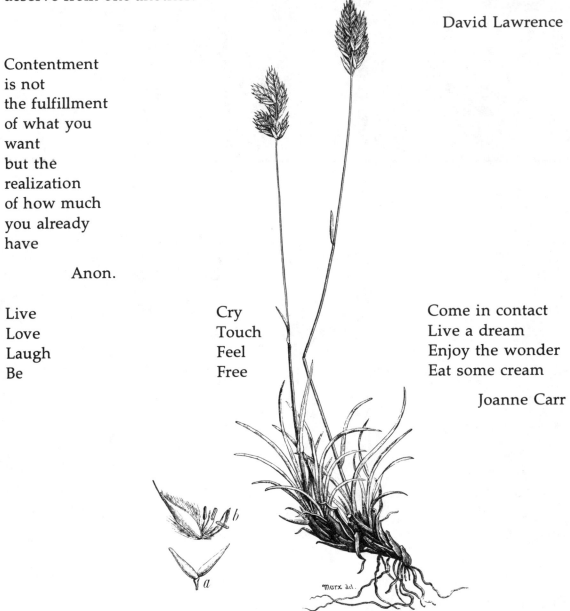

Live   Cry   Come in contact
Love   Touch   Live a dream
Laugh   Feel   Enjoy the wonder
Be   Free   Eat some cream

Joanne Carr

What we all probably know in our hearts but fail to acknowledge is that there is no perfect person awaiting our arrival and that no orgasm has much significance outside of a relationship. Each person is flawed in some way but has the potential to be a wonderful friend and lover. Each sexual experience outside of a relationship is like a whiff of poppers or a toke of grass. They frequently provide momentary pleasure but they are only a distraction from the real need to love and be loved.

Brian McNaught

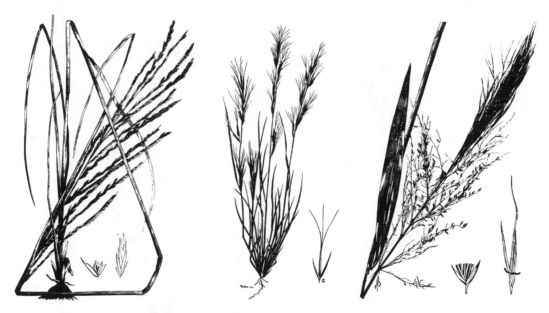

1. Don't try—do it.
2. When I push—everyone trips.
3. Life is so simple—eventually.
4. Carry your thoughts lightly.
5. There is no blame—no mistakes—only lessons.
6. Experience your own personal power and you won't have to control anyone.

Gloria and Barry Blum

I will be gentle with myself
I will love myself
I am part of the Universe
We are one together.

Joseph and Nathan

And from now on we are responsible. And accomplices.

Elie Wiesel

Knowledge can be communicated but not wisdom.

Herman Hesse

The only valid loyalty oath is
to the principle of
free inquiry.

John P. Roche

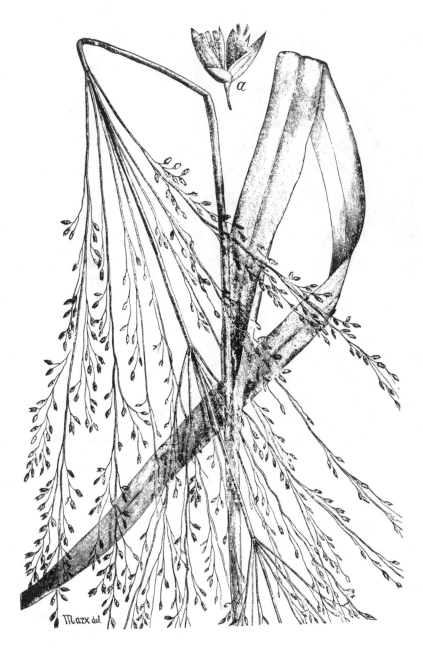

Every man's* foremost task is the actualization of his unique, unprecedented, and never-recurring potentialities, and not the repetition of something that another, and be it even the greatest, has already achieved.

Martin Buber

What man* actually needs is not a tensionless state but rather the striving and struggling for some goal worthy of him.

Viktor E. Frankl

*Both Buber and Frankl wrote at a time when it was common practice to use ''man'' to mean both sexes.

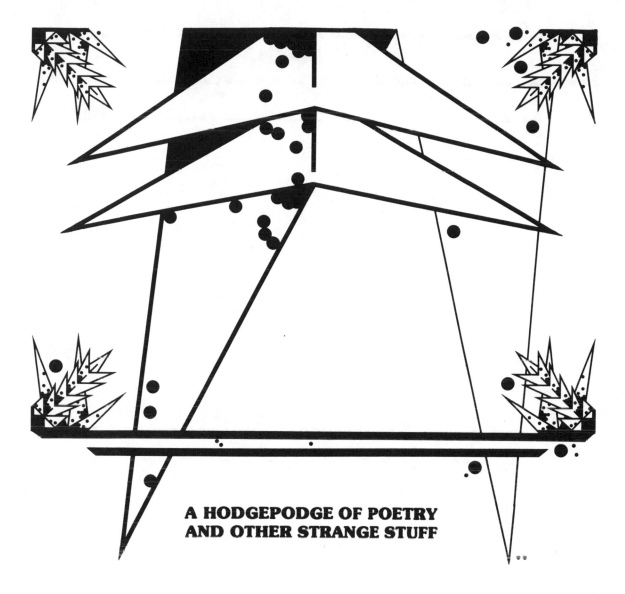

A HODGEPODGE OF POETRY AND OTHER STRANGE STUFF

Think of words . . . any words . . . that you like or that you find interesting. If you can't think of any, look in a book or magazine and pick out words that strike your fancy or that you like the sound of.

When you have written down 10 or 20, shuffle them around in any order you like and divide them up into several groups. Play around with the words in each of these groups until you get an image, a sound or an idea that interests or pleases you. Feel free to take out any words you don't want and to fit in new words (including words like "the," "that," "but," "and," "then," and so on).

Once you've gone that far, it's not too hard to arrange these words to make up the verses of a nonrhyming, free-style poem.

When you finish, turn the page to learn something you will be very interested to know. (Don't look ahead before you finish your poem, or you may spoil the experience.)

A POEM*

_____

_____

_____

_____

_____

_____

_____

_____

_____

_____

*an original by_____.

SO, YOU WROTE THE POEM...

Congratulations! You have revealed something very important about yourself to yourself. Try to figure it out.

Are you confused? It's OK. Enjoy your new creation instead.

CREATED EQUAL

everybody
is
somebody
unique
compare not
yourself
with anybody else
lest
you spoil
God's curriculum

IT'S NEVER TOO LATE

to try again
to grow again
to share again
to risk again
to feel again
to change again
to love again
to be enthusiastic again
or read
Winnie The Pooh
for the first
time.

WHAT WAS THE WORST THING THAT EVER HAPPENED TO YOU?

Now, answer this question—
What was good about it?
every mistake can become
a lesson. . . .
Even tragic events can become
lessons.
Why allow the ghosts of
the past
to determine what
you can do
today?

SURE

Sure. Sure. Sure. Sure.
Seashore. G. B. Shaw.
is sure,
was sure,
who's sure
any more?

Was Shaw
sure?
Not any more
me, sure?

Sure. Sure. Sure.
See. See. Sea. Sure.

Not any more
for sure.

CHEERLEADER *by David Ari Leavitt* *

I saw her cheering at a football game,
She was doing cartwheels in the stands.
She was smiling and looking at me,
And I was clapping my hands.

Cheerleader—you look so fine.
Cheerleader—if I played football you'd be mine.

She took me to a cheerleader party
I thought that it would never end.
She was cheerleader laughing and cheerleader smiling
With all her cheerleader friends.

Cheerleader—you dress so fine.
Cheerleader—you came off the assembly line.

I know that everyone of us is different
So why do we all try to act the same.
The cheerleaders are driving me crazy
'Cause I don't play their little game.

Cheerleader—you look so fine.
Cheerleader—if I played football you'd be mine
Cheerleader—You came off the assembly line
Cheerleader—if I played football you'd be mine.

*David was a joy of a boy—a poet, a musician and a Mensch—killed at age seventeen by a drunk driver. I publish his poem as a tribute to him and his parents who are very special friends.

47

Where Have All the Heroes Gone?

Because there are no more heroes, you have to be your own.

No, you don't agree? You can think of some heroes?

List some people you admire who struggled against overwhelming odds for a worthy cause:

1. _____
2. _____
3. _____
4. _____
5. _____
6. _____

or more

Perhaps you know some antiheroes (or, as we say in Yiddish, "schlemiels"*):

1. _____
2. _____
3. _____
4. _____
5. _____
6. _____

or more

*It goes without saying—A schlemiel is the kind of person who falls on his back and breaks his nose.

COUNTER HEROES

This is the last year of
my youth
I want to make
a thing of it.

Too bad the world is
black and white
color TV can't help us much

What are you waiting for
Indeed
death is not

I'm not ready
my Lord
ready or not
my Lord
I'm not

I'm looking for
salvation
and when I
find
it
I'll look for counter-salvation

I'm looking for
you
my love
and when I
find you
I'll look for
counter you

I'm looking for
a hero
my salvation
my love
and if I find you

I won't see you
for the forest
has become

a tree
and the
tree is not
free
to move about
like an antihero
sandwich

Amen.

KADDISH

What are you
waiting for

What force
propels you

to destroy your

beautiful body

with my perfect mind

where is your
mind

eating away

all the cream cheese
in the
neighborhood

until one
day

it was
clear
    after all the anger
and
    despair
        and the cream
cheese
    and the milk and
the beer
    and the
shoes and the shirts
and all the money
turned
    to hate
and all the love
    returned with hate
and after
    all the sleep
and the TV
    and the lies
and the contempt
    and all
        the four o'clocks in
the morning
    and the heavy drunken
climb
    up our despair
you turned into
a cream cheese
sandwich

delectable and
charming

and you said good
morning and thank you

and we flipped
with joy

and said Kaddish
to our despair

and we asked you to
clean your room
and you did.

A SNEAKY TRICK

Here's a test you can try whether you are pro-astrology, against it, or neutral. Select, at random, an astrology book that provides fairly detailed passages interpreting various zodiacal signs. Find someone who knows little about astrology but is curious about it and ask for his or her sign (as indicated by date of birth). Then tell your friend you are reading the interpretation for her/his sign—but actually read out the interpretation for a different sign, substituting words here and there as may be necessary to avoid giving away the game. (Tell her/him of your subterfuge afterward.) During the reading, note her/his reactions. Do many suggestions strike a sympathetic or responsive chord? Does s/he seem at least partly convinced? Ask her/him immediately afterward, "Would you say that this was pretty close to the mark?"

What conclusions do you draw from the experiment?

**FOR PEOPLE
WHO ARE ALLERGIC
TO IDEAS:**

FOUR AD VICES

(for people I really care about)

1. If you have a really far-out goal or even a near-in one, don't tell anyone. Work for it; don't subject it to prior review or criticism from anyone.
2. Don't think of yourself as lazy (ever). Laziness is a description, not an explanation. It's better to think of yourself as unmotivated (for the moment).
3. Repeat to yourself over and over again: Cheap is expensive; until it is clear to you that anything worthwhile (in life) is expensive.
4. If you find yourself negative and angry most of the time, it's because you feel that way about yourself. Try being nice to people. It will rub off on you (after a while).

Write your own Ad Vices for someone you care about.

WISH YOU COULD BUT KNOW YOU WON'T

I wish I could knock the shit out of people who are
   rude, like those who talk at movies or won't stop even when you ask them to
   crude, like those who throw litter around and mess up beautiful parks
or   lewd, like those who talk only in dirty jokes.

I wish I could knock the shit out of people who are
   cruel and hateful and especially those who
   mug and steal and murder because they can't get what they want.

I wish I could
   to all the mean people in the world
   but I'm afraid to try it because of what *they*
   might do to me.

 TURN IMMEDIATELY TO THE NEXT PAGE

Make up your own wish-you-could list

_____

_____

_____

_____

_____

_____

WHAT ARE YOU WAITING FOR?

ENJOY PROTECT KNOW DISCOVER BE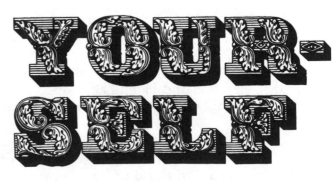

THE PSYCHOLOGY OF A REACTIONARY*

Not many people are
responsive to other people
(most react)
When you
Respond
you care about what
another person thinks
or feels
When you react
you care only about
how you feel or think

Responsive people are a joy
to be with
Reactive people are boring
or hostile

Risk letting people know
who you are
or want to be
by
Responding more and
reacting less

Even though many people do not
care about
who you are
or want to be
but have a tendency to
react more or less
reactionary.

LET IT BEGIN WITH YOU

Being unselfish
        really
        is
rarely possible
without
Getting it together
Selfishly for yourself
Really
really
Often

*This is a nonpoem with an incongruous title. It is an homage to responsive people, presented in poetic form as a tribute to my friend Craig Snyder, who started me thinking about my own reactionary tendencies.

53

Put your own favorite photos here!

THE REAL THING

The recall and retelling is
often better than what happened

The anticipation or the suspense
is often better than what happens

Some people sit around
expostulating how everything
should be

modes change our perception

People come in two kinds
Morose and optimistic
to the former
     tragic foreboding emerge easily
     the latter
     anticipations of fine events
     crowd reality

If you have money and a little imagination
everything is easier
but not always better

I DON'T TRUST PEOPLE WHO

really believe the stories they make up about the "good old days"
have the answer
are born again (without a new vision)
have found IT
boast a lot
talk too much
say they are busy
are greedy
have nothing to do
make a virtue of not being well informed
are sanctimonious
are pompous, self-righteous, smart-assed columnists
quote the Bible (selectively) to justify their own
narrow minds
are jealous
or envious
or live a life of regrets
gossip
think this country is going to the dogs
or that it belongs to them
pose as rites to life
are contemptuous of me because of my popularity
or notoriety, as the case may be

The next time somebody talks to you about the good old days, just show them this picture. (Library of Congress)

I'M NOT A GURU, ARE YOU?

If you are
        searching for
the Answer
you won't find it here.

Make you own way to
the false messiahs
true believers and new charismatics
that abound
(to find you suggestible).

My way
is to raise questions
(tell stories)
about the nature of things
and the spirit of people.

The question is

if you feed the goldfish, how
do you expect them to express
their gratitude?

or is it?

How can I find you
in the context of myself
and in the spirit of us all?

WHAT I LIKE BEST
ABOUT THE GOOD OLD DAYS
ARE ITS POEMS AND DITTIES

I

If you keep your money well
you always will have
a penny to spend
a penny to lend and
a penny for a friend.

II

One thing at a time
and that done well
is a very good rule
as many can tell.

III

The snail, she lives in a little round house
In the garden under a tree
She says, I have but a little room
But it's large enough for me.

The snail, she lives in her little round house
From year and to year's end.
You're home, Mrs. Snail, that's all very well
But you can never receive a friend.

IV

Tomorrow, tomorrow
not today
all lazy people say.

Morgen, morgen
Nur nicht heute
sagen alle faulen leute.

V

If you wish to be happy
all the day,
Make others happy,
that's the way.

VI

If you try and try and try,
And do not pout or cry,
You will find by and by
It is best to try and try.

VI

Ligeved og naesten
Slaar ingen mand af hesten

Danish proverb

"Almost or nearly doesn't throw a man off a horse"

Sometimes people come to me
and say

　　Life has no meaning. I
must go off and find myself

I reply

　　Where are you going? And
with whose money?
　　You need to find yourself
where you are
　　Then go off and "find"
someone else to discuss *it*
with.

Flowers. . . .

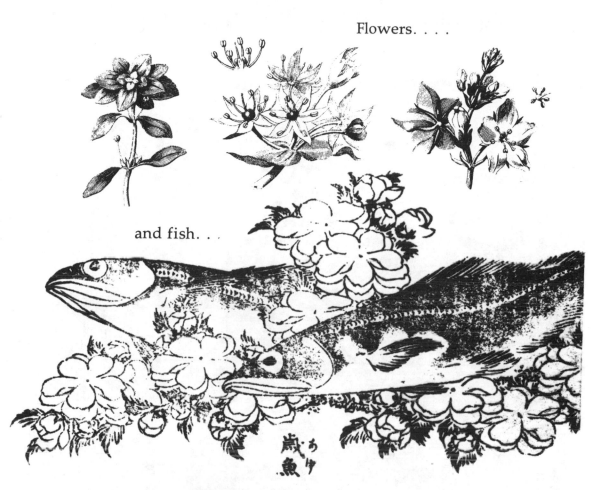

and fish. . .

make a nice dish.

TEENAGE SURVIVAL

If you can't find your way—
make your own.

SURVIVING HIGH SCHOOL

❝ You could do better if you applied yourself. **❞**

Sure, you could do better if you applied yourself. But maybe you *can't* apply yourself. Once, in desperation, I said to my son—an underachieving student—"Why don't you pay attention to your teacher?" He replied, "But, Dad, it's boring to pay attention."

I must confess that I survived my schooling by daydreaming. But my grades were so bad that I couldn't talk my way into a college for quite a while and then not even to one of my choice. If you can't pull off the daydreaming, get involved in something that's exciting and interesting to you. It doesn't matter what—drama, sports, religion. Perhaps the inspiration and the energy you acquire that way will rub off a little and give you enough patience to apply yourself to the routine, boring stuff that most schools call the compulsory curriculum. Just the same, keep in mind that the future can be counted on to provide the penalties for today's self-neglect.

❝ You'll never get a good job if you don't go to college. **❞**

A well-paying job is not the answer to life's challenge. And besides, a college degree doesn't guarantee a good education. It doesn't guarantee anything, really. On the other hand, we must recognize that there are certain jobs in this country that require a college degree. Now is the time to start asking yourself: "What kind of skills do I want to learn? Is college where I need to learn them?" Maybe you should work a few years, then go to college. Maybe not. But whatever the case, don't assume that not going to college is by itself some kind of awful failure. But don't evict yourself either. Most "interesting" jobs require a college degree before you can even apply for them.

❝ Because of your report card, you're grounded for a week. **❞**

Look, the most important thing about grades is what they can get you (and can't get you). It's tough when your parents put the pressure on, but your grades are really your business. As long as you achieve in other areas, have friends, and have lots of different things to do, bad grades don't mean that

there is something drastically wrong with you. If you are an all-around underachiever, have no friends, and also have lousy grades, you need to risk making a friend and risk achieving in some area of interest to you. Obviously the better the grade, the "lesser" the hassle. It might be worth it.

❝I just can't understand why you can't learn (English, algebra, science).**❞**

The best way to deal with a subject you are blocked in is to lay off it for a while and to develop skills in other areas. When people keep harassing you to learn a particular subject or skill, they may be making it harder for you. Try asking them politely to let you work it out yourself. It might not help, but then again it just might. Anyway, it is not the end of the world when you can't learn something. But keep in mind learning is less tiresome than not learning no matter how boring the subject matter.

❝When we were kids we took our studies seriously.
We knew it was a privilege to go to school.**❞**

In classes that are so boring that you can't handle them, sit in the back of the room and do something creative—doodle, write poems, read comic books, anything to get you through periods of meaninglessness. Sometimes (not always) you must put up with regulations and controls you don't like if you are to eventually get what you want. No point in failing, however. You'll only have to take the course over again.

Going to school shouldn't mean "going along with the system." Systems are just not where it's at. Meaning is what is important.

Still, it is certainly true that many faculty members are basically disrespectful of students while insisting that they be bowed down to (no matter what they say). All right, so many adults are immature. Some aren't. Take the good things you are offered and throw out the bad.

If you are to hold on to your self-respect and independence it is essential that you maintain a somewhat skeptical attitude. (But that doesn't mean you have to be a cynic.) Just because some High Muckamuck says something is so doesn't make it so.

Remember this: *Real knowledge is SELF-taught.*

Just the same, don't let bad classroom experiences turn you off from learning anything. How can you fulfill yourself if you are opposed to expanding you mind (and your skills)?

Get into something. Sports, drama, even politics. Some schools encourage student power such as control over student papers or even optional courses.

If nothing works, try talking your parents into paying for alternative or "free" schools or colleges. For example, point out that as it stands now, you are doing badly, so you wonder if they would be willing to help you prove yourself in a different type of environment. Most parents find "unstructured" learning distasteful, but it's worth a try.

THE REASON WHY PEOPLE HAVE DIFFICULTY LEARNING IN SOME SITUATIONS

IS THAT THEY EQUATE EDUCATION WITH SUBMISSION

For those planning to drop out of HIGH SCHOOL

Look at the box of income potentials below. Keep in mind that the lowest-paid work is usually the most dull, dehumanizing work. A system that punishes people who can't hack school isn't right, but that's the way it is.

The high school drop-outs who make good are usually very remarkable people with a lot of other things going for them. That doesn't mean you aren't a remarkable person. If your self-esteem is high, you may make it without that diploma. But don't count on it. Most employers require a high school diploma even for the most ordinary work.

If you still feel compelled to quit school, check out your state's high school equivalency program.

A LIFETIME'S EARNINGS: THE IMPACT OF EDUCATION

Estimated total income from age 18 to death for males* with varying levels of education

Less than 8 years	$500,000
Grade school completed	$600,000
High school—1 to 3 years	$700,000
High school completed	$900,000
College—1 to 3 years	$1,000,000
College completed	$1,400,000
College—5 years or more	$1,700,000

*For females, the figures in each category are several thousand dollars less.

SURVIVING COLLEGE

For those planning to go to college and for those already there:

Half the people who start college drop out before finishing. *Their reasons for quitting have little to do with intellectual ability.* (Plenty of semiliterate, badly educated, poorly trained people are graduated from our universities every year.)

College can be an *opportunity* to teach yourself in an environment of concentrated intellectual resources and stimulating company. But people who haven't discovered that they must dig out the gold themselves from the vast mountain of slag that is also part of college are easily disillusioned and discouraged.

The biggest reasons for quitting are unhappiness due to not making friends and to uninteresting courses, as well as financial problems.

The person who is not used to being out of his/her crowd and away from family will have a rough time if s/he tends to be lonely and isolated anyway. Listen, if you have no friends and you aren't the super-studious type and you can't hack the sorority/fraternity trip—what's left? Without the stimulation of good company even your few interesting courses tend to become meaningless. You need to go out of your way to take chances to make even one or two friends (apart from chatting with the people in your dorm). Get off your duff and make a point of going out for the evening. At the campus flick or the local hangout sit near someone else who is alone. You'd be surprised how conversations can develop out of a remark about the flick or the food. An excellent method of finding meaningful relationships is to *volunteer* at the campus crisis center, health service, or student association. Everybody is always pleading for volunteers. Make yourself useful. This is a good way to make friends.

FRESHMEN BEWARE

After you go through the agonizing experiences of getting organized and registered, you are likely to find—if you attend an ordinary college—that freshmen are systematically frozen and manipulated out of all the interesting courses.

As a psychologist and a professor, I can tell you, for example, that on most campuses the introductory psych course has almost nothing to do with what psychologists actually do when they work with people. I sometimes suspect that, because psychology is attractive to many students, the first courses in psych are made as boring as possible to eliminate everyone but the super-studious types.

Other people professions are the same. For example, the reason there are so few humanistically oriented physicians around is that aspiring doctors have to go through a tedious dehumanizing curriculum.

There are exceptions, of course. For example, several psychiatrists I know hardly ever use anything from their early training, but they feel that they had to pay the price.

The price? If you want to get into psychology or medicine or social work or some other allied profession and you basically care about people even though you are a scientist, *you just have to suffer*.

DON'T FORGET:

You can always try transferring. There are lots of colleges with considerable curriculum freedom that is reflected in a more liberal atmosphere.

Many people who have failed at one school have made good after they were fortunate enough, or clever enough, to make an appropriate transfer.

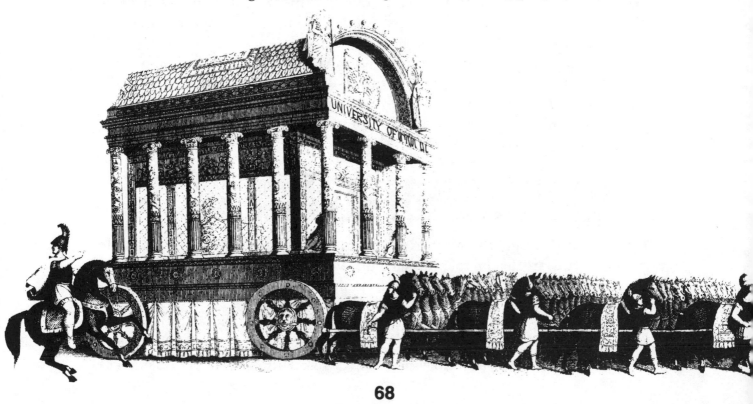

RECOMMENDED NOVELS

Here is a list of the novels I've read that have had the greatest impact on me—all of which I read with enormous excitement, even if I can't say they would all (even most) make any scholar's "best" list. Many of my readers under twenty-five probably will not have ever heard of the majority of them.

The eighteen (listed here not exactly in order of "impact") are:

1. *Jean Christopher.* Romain Rolland.
2. *The Brothers Karamazov.* Fyodor Dostoyevsky.
3. *Buddenbrooks.* Thomas Mann.
4. *Three Cities.* Sholem Asch.
5. *Billy Budd.* Herman Melville.
6. *U.S.A.* John Dos Passos.
7. *The Stranger.* Albert Camus.
8. *Amerika.* Franz Kafka.
9. *Three Lives.* Gertrude Stein.
10. *Man's Fate.* Andre Malraux.
11. *Orlando.* Virginia Wolfe.
12. *Razor's Edge.* Somerset Maugham.
13. *Brideshead Revisited.* Evelyn Waugh.
14. *Herzog.* Saul Bellow.
15. *Moby Dick.* Herman Melville.
16. *An Unofficial Rose.* Iris Murdoch.
17. *The Mayor of Casterbridge.* Thomas Hardy.
18. *Night.* Elie Wiesel.

Now, Some Non·Fiction

The Way of Man According to the Teaching of Hasidism
Martin Buber • The Citadel Press

Love Is Letting Go of Fear
Gerald G. Jampolsky • Celestial Arts

Man's Search for Meaning
Viktor E. Frankl • Pocket Books

A Jew Today
Elie Wiesel • Vintage Books

The Lazy Man's Guide to Enlightenment
Thaddeus Golas • Bantam Books

A Time for Being Human
Eugene Kennedy • Cornerstone Library

I Touch the Earth, the Earth Touches Me
Hugh Prather • Doubleday and Company

The Survivors—an Anatomy of Life in the Death Camps
Terrence Des Pres • Pocket Books

To Have or To Be
Erich Fromm • Harper and Row

Drawing on the Right Side of the Brain
Betty Edwards • J. P. Tarcher, Inc.

Embodiment—an Approach to Sexuality and Christian Theology
James B. Nelson • Augsburg Publishing House

The Good Old Days—They Were Terrible!
Otto L. Bettmann • Random House

A few recent novels that are exciting to me

Ragtime by E. L. Doctorow
The World According to Garp by John Irving
Jailbird by Kurt Vonnegut
The Prince of Tides by Pat Conroy
The Women of Brewster Place by Gloria Naylor

The people on this page don't want you to read this book.

Donald Wildmon
Jerry Falwell
Phyllis Schlafly

71

WHAT YOU SHOULD KNOW ABOUT ROUTINE WORK YOU HATE

We all have to do varying amounts of tedious, mechanical, and, often, unfulfilling work.

Here is one way to tell whether you should do it: If you don't do it, will you feel bad (like less of a person)? Or will you feel better?

If you are having a hard time getting the work done that you need to do, maybe you need to develop endurance. Endurance is what keeps you going despite pain and fatigue. If you want to learn about endurance, try setting yourself the goal of walking, or jogging, twice as far as you've ever walked or jogged, and then do it, allowing yourself no excuses. (By the way, have you ever noticed how easy it is to get aches and pains and an upset stomach when you face doing something you don't want to do?)

Sometimes you can do something that you hate doing by not fighting it and getting into a rhythm. Usually you get the rhythm as you move along, not before you start.

If you have a big pile of monotonous work to do, schedule it in stages. If you leave it all for one big session you probably will end up not doing it at all. Even so, doing it in one big all-nighter is better than not even trying.

There may be some types of work that you shouldn't be doing. Suppose you go to work for a boss who is almost always ruthless and dishonest with his customers. The work you are doing is helping your boss be a crook. Maybe you should take a stand.

Remember: *If you don't do the monotonous work that needs to be done, all your pleasurable experiences are reduced to cop-outs.* (Of course, some people use work as their main way of avoiding their problems. That's a drag, too.)

WHAT YOU SHOULD KNOW ABOUT JOBS

If you want to get a devastating picture of work, read Studs Terkel's *Working*. He shows that almost nobody likes his/her job. And of the few people who do like their work, most of them had to wait years before they found such a spot.

The point is that there are *very few* entry points into the work world that give *real* job satisfaction. The fact is that most jobs are a drag.

But it is really good if you can get work that you like. Yet, if you can't, you have several options:

(1) Take advantage of your leisure time by being with friends and family and by accomplishing things that don't have much, if any, financial payoff.

(2) Work extra hard to get money. However, be sure to think this over: How important is money in your life? What exactly do you plan to use it for? We're not against making money, but too many breadwinners have sacrificed family, friends and leisure for an extra buck. In this regard, when you get older be cautious about making a change that might look good, but not be worth it. Many marriages have been shaken and some have been wrecked after a promotion tied to transfer to a new community with a different, high-pressure life-style. Additionally, that new promotion may turn out to be a completely inappropriate place for someone with your skills, talents and inclinations. People have stayed in one job for years, and then, two or three months after being promoted, have quit or been fired.

(3) If you want to improve your job situation, be aware that once you have a position, your chances of success most often hinge on enthusiasm, your own initiative (ideas), and—many people don't realize this—your willingness to take care of details. "Idea" people are a dime a dozen, and so are "details" people. Whether you work on your own or for an employer, your services are usually highly prized when you are able to get things done by not only thinking something up, but also by wrapping up the hundreds of uninteresting details. (It doesn't always turn out this way, of course. You may end up under a boss who feels threatened by your competence.)

UNEMPLOYMENT

If you simply can't find work, consider self-employment. It has its ups and downs and insecurity, but at least you have more opportunity to make up some of your own rules of the game.

Of course, if you think that you can or should do only one type of work, you narrow down your possibilities to free-lance.

Whatever you do, don't let "unemployed" time become dead time. After all, working or not, it's still your life going by. Rather than sitting around thinking (or complaining) about how rotten life is, or going from bar to bar or from bed to TV set, use the time to learn a new skill, to read, to catch up on all the little things you've been putting off.

COMPETITION

Finally, understand that competition is somewhat important, but don't let it drive you into a mental hospital or to the grave.

You'd be amazed at how worried and obsessed people get about "success." Certainly you need to succeed. But first, you simply must ask yourself what that word means *for you.* If you constantly compare yourself to what others are doing and making, you will be unbelievably miserable.

Really, you need to be thinking about what are and what should be the most important elements in your life.

COPING WITH YOUR PARENTS

There are many kids living at home who get along with their parents; some have been able all along and some have struggled to reach this point. That's fine!

This part is for those of you who are not doing too well because you feel your parents are either:

☐too strict ☐too old fashioned ☐too opinionated

☐too prying ☐too smart ☐not smart enough ☐too busy ☐not busy enough

☐too sarcastic ☐smothering ☐not understanding enough

☐too observant (they think they know or notice everything you do)

Let's face it, all parents are old-fashioned—especially those who claim that they are modern. Starting with the premise of having old-fashioned parents will help you develop strategies of getting along. This is essential at some

75

time, because kids who don't come to an understanding with their parents are haunted by them, often through their entire lives. Even though they are determined never to be like their parents, as adults they imitate their parents' worst traits. The exception to this general rule is the kid who is genuinely more mature than his/her parents. These particular kids need to free themselves from parental influence as soon as possible and eventually to learn to understand and love—if not respect—their parents.

In the final analysis everyone needs to become reasonably independent. Thus you are in a strong position to cope with parents only if you are working toward independence for yourself.

This means
    You have strong interests of your own and
    You are working toward a goal.
It could be:

▶ Going to college (even if you have no idea of what your major is going to be).

▶ Earning your own living (in a career of *your* choice, not of your parents').

▶ Wanting to live on a farm (even if your parents ridicule the idea).

▶ Planning to become an artist (even if you're expected to join the family business).

You cannot have any "claims" on your parents if your response to them is avoidance of responsibilities or if your relationship to them is hostile-dependent (meaning you can't get along with them or without them).

Here is a formula for successful coping with your parents. The odds are that what we're going to suggest *won't* work for you. (You didn't expect that, did you?) The gimmick here is that working in the right direction will eventually offer you the independence you will want *even if* your current family situation does not improve much. If you can hack our advice, your situation will improve. The problem is, of course, that you can't expect your parents to change much—but your attitudes toward them can change drastically.

Here goes . . .

The one-month politeness campaign—which can be especially effective when you want something badly (a car, a trip, more money, almost anything except permission for premarital sex or a motorcycle).

Make it a point to be very polite without being sarcastic.

It takes a bit of faking it.

You must be able to say at appropriate times:

- Good morning.
- Thank-you.
- I appreciate your doing "it" for me.
- I'm sorry, I didn't mean to upset you.

(and, if possible, at least once a week without being asked):

I'll be glad to take out the garbage.

I'll be glad to help clean up.

Can I get anything for you? or, Is there anything I can do for you? I have half an hour to spare.

I'll be glad to stay home with so-and-so (a younger sibling).

Chances are, your parents will flip.

You might even overhear them ask each other if they should send you to a psychiatrist.

The main thing is not to fall into any traps they set. Their response might be:

(1) You want something from us. (Your polite response: "Of course. You always said I should work for something I wanted.")

(2) Some snide remark like: "What's gotten into you?" or "Now you want to be helpful . . . where have you been all my life?" (Your response: "I haven't been very considerate before. I'm trying to change to see if being considerate will get me anywhere.")

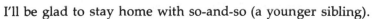

MOMMA   By Mell

77

After a month, ask for what you want in this way:

"I'd like to talk to you about something, but I would appreciate it if your first response is not 'No.' "

Chances are fifty-fifty you won't get what you want—you may have to extend the campaign.

You may discover in the process that politeness makes things much easier for you, even if you didn't get what you wanted. In any case it is extremely important to know that politeness is not a method for getting closer to your parents; it is a way of establishing a distance that permits you to discover your own way. You may want to use the distance as an opportunity to get closer, but that's up to you.

 These are courtesies appreciated by most parents:

- Make it a point (or a sacrifice) to spend a couple of hours a week with your parents. Talk to them about anything, or just watch TV with them, but be sure to talk to them during the commercials.
- Every once in a while ask a parent who works outside the home: "How are things going?" (and if s/he says "Fine," say: "I mean, I'd like to hear about your job/business.")
- Not too often—perhaps a couple of times a month—ask one or both parents for their advice about something not too crucial so you can occasionally follow their suggestions.
- Experiment with telling the truth every once in a while—but start by saying: "I worry that if I tell you the truth you'll be very upset" or "When I tell the truth, the whole thing gets blown up out of proportion."
- Clean up your room at unexpected times.
- Praise them for things they do well.

THINGS NOT TO DO:

- Don't ever announce your good intentions, such as: "I'm going to study all weekend." Instead, say, after the fact: "I was surprised at how much I accomplished."
- Don't say, "You don't understand me." No parent can handle it. Say instead: "I guess it's been difficult for me to explain myself to you" or "I feel badly that I have not been able to help you understand me."
- Don't send cards or cheap presents to your parents on birthdays, holidays, etc. Instead, try to do something original like preparing a meal and cleaning up afterward, writing a poem, or making something on you own.
- Don't tell your parents you're in love until it's lasted a couple of months unless you want to risk being made fun of or humiliated. If anything, understate your interest in the other person.

With rare exceptions, parents don't expect much from their kids these days, so they are really quite easy to please.

The best way to think of your parents is
(First and Foremost):
    They mean well
(Last but not Least):
    Their good intentions will not always lead you where you want to go.

ONE OF THE MOST DIFFICULT PROBLEMS
FOR SOME PEOPLE TO FACE IS THE FACT THAT
THEIR PARENTS ARE REALLY NICE PEOPLE.

THIS PAGE IS FOR PARENTS

(AND OTHER ADULTS)

Expressions guaranteed to turn off young people:

1. I want to have a serious talk with you.
2. We trust you.
3. When I was your age . . .
4. Because we say so.
5. As long as I don't know about it.
6. Act your age.
7. It's about time you (got good grades, straightened your room . . .)
8. Just a minute.
9. Ask your father/mother.
10. Are you telling me the truth?
11. That's not your idea, is it?
12. Don't you dare talk to me that way.
13. Get off your high horse.
14. Wipe that smile off your face.
15. What will the neighbors say . . .?
16. After all we've done for you . . .

And in response to a love affair:

17. You'll get over it.
18. When you get older, you'll laugh about it yourself.
19. It's puppy love.
20. Of course you can't take out the garbage, you're in love.
21. Don't do anything I wouldn't do.
22. Where did we go wrong?

For Teenagers Whose Parents Are
About To Be Or Who Have Recently Become

Obviously, you can't—and shouldn't—eliminate all your grief and guilt, but know this:

**Children are almost never responsible
for the break-up of a marriage!**

So stay off the heavy guilt, self-punishment trip (which is always harmful).

Stifling your feelings to please a parent usually does more harm than good. In general, the best policy is one of enlightened self-interest.

As a teenager, you have a right to make some decisions, including having some say about which parent you live with. It shouldn't be a matter of custody, but of choice. Talking these things over isn't easy, but it's important for you to struggle to have a voice in the decision-making process. Your decision should be based on your needs rather than on feeling sorry for a parent. If you are able to do this, you won't fall into the trap of "taking sides" and assigning blame (which is a bummer). In this respect, you may want to say, "I'd like to live with *you* for a while, *but* I'd like to have the right to change my mind if, after a year or so, it doesn't work out."

If necessary, you may have to start out by saying, "I know this upsets you, but my intent is to protect myself, rather than try to please somebody. . ."

This idea of enlightened self-interest can also be carried over to your brothers and sisters. It might be a good idea for all of you to discuss it among yourselves and then for each of you to decide whom you would like to live with. The idea that all of you should stay together *at any cost* is foolish. Maybe yes, maybe no.

If one of your parents has died,
read the section on Death—especially
the part about guilt.

If you've spent most of your life with one parent, you should know that one in three adult Americans is currently not married to anyone. Single adults number around 43 million in this country.

Of course, you may have to accept certain defeats and some unpleasant limitations (such as visitation hassles). Some decisions will be beyond your control. Sometimes there is no fair and just way to settle these matters.

There are many reasons why it seems better to have a mother and a father living in the same home as you do—at least until you are eighteen. But it's better only if both parents usually get along with each other.

Remembering that it's too much of a strain not to ventilate your feelings and talk things out, you may be able to help your parent not feel sorry or deprived by suggesting something like:

"It's bad enough not having two parents around—why make it harder by feeling sorry for yourself? Let's see how we can help each other."

or

"I can't take the place of the missing parent and I don't want to. I want to remain your child, even if it does mean added responsibilities."

or

Reassure your parent that you like it better without the tension that may have been an overbearing part of his/her married state.

So even if you accept that the whole thing is tragic, *the worst thing that you can do is to feel sorry for yourself.* If you go around feeling ashamed of your family's status, you'll find the pressure of covering up that shame to be enormous. For example, when someone asks you about your parents, you try to avoid discussion. It would be much better to simply say, "They're divorced (or separated)." The first few times, you may find it difficult to admit it, but what a relief it is to be able to speak freely. Don't compare your situation unfavorably with anyone else's. It's surprising how often the intact, wonderful family across the street, that you've admired and felt jealous about, falls apart without warning.

Be aware that everyone has troubles. One family has a retarded child, another has children and doesn't want them, other families can't make ends meet, while many families are not satisfied despite great affluence.

In spite of everything, most kids like their families—even though there are times when they don't. The fact that your family is not a currently conventional one should not make much difference in the long run, especially if you don't use your "orphan" status as a cop-out. Remember too, only 12% of American families consist of a father-breadwinner, mother stay-at-home with two children.

All really meaningful experiences are of brief duration (which can be repeated).

Mature Love* is . . .

. . . when your caring about the other person is *just a little* more important to you than having the other person care for you. The relationship is mutually enhancing and energizing.

Immature Love is . . .

. . . when the relationship is one–sided or very imbalanced. Your love is a burden on the other person and the state of being in love is exhausting.

It's too bad that many people think that when they find true love "everything will be perfect." They think that there must not be any disagreements and that each partner will always want to be with the other. When a problem comes up they are likely to end the relationship thinking that "love has died." Then they go off looking for someone else with whom they can experience "the real thing." As a result, they find every relationship a disappointment, and they may wonder why no one seems to be as sensitive as they are.

Sometimes people say and believe that they are in love, but they act in a way that is sure to sabotage the relationship. They neglect their studies or their work; or they're careless about their appearance; or they're jealous, irritable, and petty when they are with the other person; or they fail to keep promises or assume the obligations that are common when two people really love each other.

People who are in love will be so intent on making themselves the best possible partner for the loved one that they are inspired to improve their work, to enhance their appearances and to show the best side of their

*In this context we are referring to responsive love: being aware and concerned about the impact your love has on others. Love can start out as mature, and degenerate into a nightmare by becoming possessive, stifling, or controlling. It can, of course, start out immature and become mature.

personalities. The true lover tries in every way possible to make him/herself a better person, so that s/he will be worthy of the love that is desired.

Real love is best when it's a shared experience. It sometimes happens that a man falls in love with a woman who does not return his feeling (or vice versa). When this happens to a mature person, s/he makes every reasonable effort to evoke affection from the other person. If this fails, s/he will be disappointed, but after a while will admit that s/he can't have what s/he wants, and will seek out another relationship.

It is not true that "really" being in love is something that can happen only once in a lifetime. It is possible to be in love many times. Even an intense love affair, when it comes to an end, may be followed by another relationship that is even more deeply rooted and more satisfying.

DO YOU WANT TO BE A LOVER?

If you were loved and taken care of as a child you will be in the best position to love and care for others. If that part of your life was not exactly the way you wanted it to be, try (in this order):

1. To care for and love yourself.

2. To care for and love, or be close to, people of your own sex. These are the best preparations for learning to:

3. Love and care for people of the opposite sex.

Once you are able to develop all three, they remain part of your life forever, and you are ready to:

4. Love and care for your children.

It's no accident that people who reject relationships with members of their own sex or who go out of their way to be with members of the opposite sex (like the woman who says: "I don't care to relate to women; they bore me" or the man who says "Man, I love women; I need to be with a woman all the time") are rarely able to establish a meaningful, mature, and lasting relationship with a member of the opposite sex.

How can you tell the difference between mature love and infatuation? For the first couple of weeks you can't. Love and infatuation are merged. After that, if the relationship takes on signs of becoming immature, it was an infatuation.

ON BEING INTIMATE WITH A CHESTNUT

Sometimes we talk about intimacy. We quickly agree that people can be sexual without being intimate. But, ah, can anyone be intimate without sex? Perhaps, but what about intimacy without touching?

We decide that there are many different levels and intensities, like in love or enchantment. The intimacy we care about seems to be being at one with, at any one moment, in harmony with:

another person
　　　an imaginary friend
　　　　　God
　　　　　　　nature
　　　　　　　　　a stuffed animal
　　　　　　　　　　a real dog
　　　　　　　　　　　your family
　　　　　　　　　　a doll
　　　　　　　　　　　Jesus
　　　　　　　　　　　　your horse
　　　　　　　　　　　　　your genitals
　　　　　　　　　　　　　　your motorcycle
　　　　　　　　　　　　　a blanket
　　　　　　　　　　　　　grass
　　　　　　　　　　　　　　　　yourself
　　　　　　　　　　　　　　　even a chestnut

It's not easy, this intimacy business. One thing we know for sure is that the path to its fulfillment can be treacherous. First you must reveal yourself. But when you do, you risk humiliation or betrayal. But you also have a chance of a response that you want. Intimacy means being responsive, not reactive.

A person falls in love with you.

God is revealed.

The motorcycle sends out vibrations.

Your doll, dog, or horse listens to you as no one else has before.

Or your music captures the soul.

Most people are afraid of being intimate.

Some people don't even know how to be.
    What a pity!
How can you tell about intimacy?

It is joyous
and sad

It is sharing and giving,
and open-ended and
taking your mind off yourself
momentarily

Have you ever touched anyone with your body or mind?
And then someone talked about being intimate with a chestnut. For an entire summer he fondled, confided in, and loved her. The response of the chestnut was simply marvelous to behold.

GETTING TO KNOW SOMEBODY IS THE ULTIMATE AROUSAL

Everyone likes the idea of being in love. Even so, they may have
many questions like:

How can you tell if it's really love?
Can you fall in love more than once?
Is love blind?
Can you love more than one person at a time?
How important is sex in a relationship?
Does love happen at first sight?
He (she) is mean to me but keeps telling me he (she) loves me. How is
    that possible?
If you have disagreements, does it mean you're not in love?

Text: Sol Gordon and Kathleen Everly
Cover Design: Vivien Cohen
Inside Illustrations: Jeff Catlett
Mechanicals: Ron Martin

Published by Ed-U Press, Inc.
P.O. Box 583
Fayetteville, NY 13066

Other titles in this series of educational comic books include *Ten
Heavy Facts About Sex, VD Claptrap, Protect Yourself From Becoming An Unwanted Parent*, and *Juice Use -- Special Hangover Edition*.
These titles and *How Can You Tell If You're Really in Love?* are
available for $1.50 each from Ed-U Press, Inc. Bulk rates upon
request.

What Is Love?

There are many different kinds of love. You can love your parents, music, your dog, and friends. However, being "in love" usually refers to a powerful desire to be with and to win the affection and respect of one other person.

If you feel you are in love, you are, but our experience is that there are two kinds:

● Mature love is when caring about the other person is just a little more important than having the other person care for you. This kind of relationship makes both partners feel better. Mature love is playful, passionate, sensitive and proud. Both partners have a lot of energy.

● Immature love is when it is much more important to have the other person care for you than it is for you to care for the other person. This kind of relationship often feels like a burden. It is exhausting because it involves more taking than giving. There is a lot of jealousy, bickering, meanness and apologies.

How Can You Tell?

You can always spot a mature couple. They have time for most all the things they have to do, like household tasks, homework and other jobs. In fact, they even have energy to enjoy themselves after they finish what they are supposed to do.

If a couple is tired or upset most of the time (whether together or apart), this is a sure sign of an immature relationship. Another sign is constantly boasting "I'm in love, I'm in love, I'm in love." This kind of person also tires out everyone else who listens.

Infatuation or Love?

There is a difference between "infatuation" and "love." In the first couple weeks of the relationship they're the same. But after that, there's a big difference. If it's infatuation, a short time after a couple gets to know each other better, the love starts to go sour or even bitter for at least one person. When it's real love, getting to know each other is a real turn-on. The relationship deepens and improves for both.

Will it Last?

Sometimes a person falls in love with someone who does not return that feeling. Mature people will make reasonable efforts to encourage affection from the other person. Of course, they feel badly if it fails, but they are also able to accept disappointments.

It is not true that "really" being in love is something that can happen only once in a lifetime. It is possible to be in love many times. Even if an intense love affair ends, it may be followed by another relationship that is even more satisfying.

Is It Getting Worse

Some people believe that they are in love but act in ways which spoil the relationship. They may neglect their studies or their work, be careless about how they look, be jealous or irritable or petty when they are with each other, and fail to keep promises. They say things like "Why didn't you call me last night?" "I saw you flirting with so and so" and "You don't love me."

or better?

People who are truly in love want to be the best partner possible. They try to improve their work and appearance. They show the best side of their personalities. They mainly feel happy when they are with each other but they can manage quite well when they are alone. This doesn't mean they never fight, but most of the time they want to please each other.

Promises, Promises

Immature love affairs are heavy with promises like "Don't worry, honey, when we get married I'll stop fooling around." Don't you believe it! A bad situation is made worse by marriage.

When immature people marry, they pay more attention to their work, sports, cars, or alcohol than they do to their partner. This doesn't mean that mature partners spend all their time together or avoid friends or their work. It's simply that their feelings for each other are more important than their jobs or their hobbies.

People who are really in love can accept that everyone has problems, makes mistakes, and is unhappy at times.

Do you really love me?
Do You Really?

Immature lovers can't stand being apart and usually have a hard time getting along when together. They often fight and argue. Everything the partner does becomes a test of love. If your partner keeps asking you "Do you love me? Do you really love me?" -- say "No". You might have your first real conversation this way.

There's another thing which sometimes fouls up relationships. It's when one partner always calls the shots and the other person just goes along. One partner asks "What do you want to do tonight?" and the other says, "Oh, anything you want to do." This kind of thing really gets to be a drag. No matter who plays what role, it's exhausting to be with someone who constantly relies on you. Mature partners have shared *and* individual interests.

HATE

Some people don't know the difference between love and hate. They write letters like

Dear Doctor Cure All,
Please help me. My husband beats me, throws food on the floor when he doesn't like it, and goes out with other women. But he says he really loves me. What should I do?

The answer is "Leave him, you idiot! That's not love, that's hate."
Some even say "She's just like her mother" or blame a nationality like "He gets wild - but you know how it is - he's Italian...Black...Jewish...Greek...Irish... They kid themselves by making up excuses for behavior that is not excusable.

Jealousy

People in immature relationships often think that jealousy is a sign of love. We think it's a signal to *stop!* We are not talking about once-in-a-while jealousy. This happens to most people. The kind of jealousy that's harmful is when it's the main worry.

All that jealousy measures is how unsure a person is. Most of the energy that jealous people have goes into trying to gain control over their partner. How exhausting.

Love is
Sharing Feelings

Of course, some relationships start out immature and become mature, as well as the opposite. We also know that both immature and mature love can be exciting and, at other times, confusing or upsetting. Most people, however, know in a short while whether the relationship is rewarding or a burden.

Like everything else in life that's worthwhile, relationships are a mix of hard work, patience, and joy. The best idea is to start sharing feelings from the beginning. Try to discuss each other's good and bad points without hurting each other. Even getting out some anger isn't bad.

...hard work and compromise

In good relationships, there has to be some give and take. Love does not grow when one person controls another. Sometimes it just makes more sense to give in, even if you think your ideas are better.

No One Can Make You Feel

Inferior . . . . .

People who care about themselves are attractive to some other people -- period. They send out signals that
- they do not need to be loved or approved of by all the people they know in order to feel important, and that
- they are not available for being used by others.

Without Your Consent

People who hate themselves and express it in being (not looking) unattractive or short-sighted tend to repel rather than attract others. If you feel that you're nobody unless somebody loves you, you probably won't amount to much even after someone loves you -- if you get that far.

Believing that certain perfumes, hair tonics, vaginal sprays or "lines" will make you "attractive" will get you nowhere. No deodorant can substitute for feeling good about yourself. Being a real person is what is attractive these days.

Sex Should Never be a Test of Love

Even people in love may have problems with sex. Sex in a mature relationship is voluntary and often takes time to become generally pleasurable. In an immature relationship, sex is exploitative, rarely enjoyable, and usually degrading.

Sex is *never a test of love*. Don't be fooled by lines like "But honey, everyone is doing it" or "If you really loved me, you'd have sex with me." People who are really in love don't put this kind of pressure on each other. Women who fall for lines usually are abandoned by the men who are using them.

Some people seem to be attracted only to parts of people. They say look at

        her breasts
        his chest
        her or his ass

This is silly. You can't have a conversation with an ass   (even a smart ass).

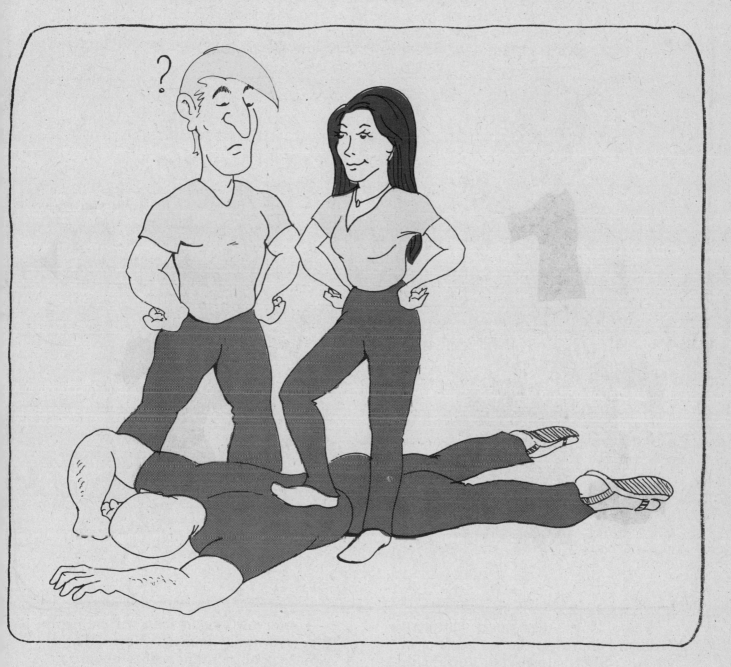

And some people show off a good looking partner. They do this because it makes them feel more attractive and important. A relationship based mostly on "showing off," however, usually doesn't last very long.

Understanding Women These Days

These days the smart, attractive women believes in the women's movement. She supports equal opportunities for career choice, leisure time, and decision making in addition to equal pay for equal work.

Today's smart woman marries for love -- not for sex, status, money, or because Mom and Dad want to be grandparents.

Tomorrow's smart man will be happier with today's smart woman. These women and men know that liberation has nothing to do with who works in or outside of the home. They also know that liberation has to do with equal opportunities, not with whether women or men are the same. Liberated people do not live in the past -- they believe in flexible roles for both men and women.

The Ten Most Important Parts of
Marriage

1. Love, sensitivity and respect for each other
2. A sense of humor and playfulness
3. Honest communication without violating private thoughts and experiences
4. Doing meaningful things together
5. Sharing time with people who are really enjoyed, either together or singly
6. Not compromising who you are or want to be, or what you want to have, like children, a career, or faithfulness to each other
7. Tolerance for weak spots (like being tired, clumsy, irritable at times) and for opposite points of view
8. Acceptance of each other's likes and dislikes, and levels of energy
9. Sexual intercourse
10. Sharing household tasks

What else do you think is important?

11.
12.
13.
14.
15.
16.
17.
18.

SIGNS OF
Immature Love

* You are tired most of the time
* Love seems more like a burden than a joy
* Violence is part of the relationship
* You keep having thoughts like "Maybe things will get better"
* Your partner frequently makes promises that aren't kept
* You feel

MISERABLE

SIGNS OF
Mature Love

* You have a lot of energy
* You have a sense of humor
* You really appreciate each other's ideas
* Neither of you *frequently* asks "Are you sure you love me?" "Do you really care about me?"
* When you are together, you spend most of your time enjoyably and creatively
* You can talk about each other's likes and dislikes
* You are a person, not a sex object
* You can spend a day alone with your partner (without television) and find it

FANTASTIC

0-934978-10-7

An ounce of PREVENTION...

Every year, almost ten million Americans are infected with sexually transmitted diseases. More than half of these victims are between the ages of 15 and 24. Many young people between the ages of 11 and 14 are also known to have VD.

Herpes alone now affects about 20 million Americans. Though the dangers of this disease have been somewhat exaggerated, it is a health hazard for many young people. As of 1986 no cure exists for herpes, though there are treatments to help lessen its symptoms.

Several forms of VD have become more widespread in the past several years. One is chlamydia, an organism which causes much of the NGU in men and the vaginitis in women. Antibiotics are used to treat it.

AIDS (Acquired Immune Deficiency Syndrome) is a fatal viral disease (HTLV-111). It first appeared in the U.S. in 1979 among homosexual men and intravenous drug users. It is spread only through unprotected sexual relations (especially anal sex), transfusions of infected blood (now almost eliminated through special screening), by a mother with the disease infecting her unborn child and the sharing of needles. AIDS is spreading to heterosexuals as a consequence of promiscuous sex and relations with bi-sexual men. In Africa, and in some countries, the disease is found predominantly among heterosexuals.

Persons in the high risk groups mentioned above must consider safe sex which absolutely demands no exchange of body fluids, particularly semen. Use of condoms and exploration of other ways of expressing affection - hugging, massaging, matual masturbation and dry kissing. Despite some progress in treatment, no cure has been found for this terrible disease.

Symptoms associated with AIDS are swollen lymph glands, unexplained bleeding, weight loss, persistent fatigue, diarrhea, dry cough and painless, purplish bumps or spots on the body.

TEXT: Sol Gordon
Facilitator: Kathleen G. Everly
Illustration and design: Roger Conant

Published by Ed-U Press
Box 583
Fayetteville, N.Y. 13066

Other titles in this series of educational comic books include: *How Can You Tell If You're Really in Love?*, *Ten Heavy Facts About Sex*, *Protect Yourself* and *Juice Use—Special Hangover Education*. These titles and VD Claptrap are available for $1.50 each from Ed-U Press. Bulk rates available.

Revised 1987 ©1973, Ed-U Press, Inc.

HOW YOU CATCH VD

Most people today refer to venereal disease as STD (Sexually Transmitted Diseases) because they are spread through sexual contact.

The most dangerous sexually transmitted diseases are gonorrhea, syphilis, AIDS and chlamydia.

Sexually transmitted germs live in warm, moist places -- such as the penis or vagina, the rectum, and the mouth. These germs travel from one person's genitals (or rectum or mouth) after direct contact with someone else's genitals (or rectum or mouth). This could mean a man and woman, two women, or two men.

③

If you didn't already know: Whether or not a person has pleasurable feelings during the sex act has nothing to do with whether s/he catches VD.

HEALTH ALERT

Due to the AIDS crisis, anal and oral sex are not considered safe, especially for homosexuals, bisexuals and their partners. Anal and vaginal intercourse and oral sex should be avoided by heterosexuals who are unsure of the fidelity of their sexual partners or whose partners are intravenous drug users.

The gonorrhea germ is very catching. In fact, the common cold is the only disease more catching than the clap.

Gonorrhea usually shows up in men two to six days after sexual contact with the person who has it, although it sometimes doesn't show up for a month or more.

The first sign is usually pus dripping from the penis or a burning feeling while urinating. However, about 10 per cent of the men who get the clap show no signs at all. Just the same, the disease can be spreading through their bodies and anyone who has sex with them is likely to catch gonorrhea.

Signs of gonorrhea disappear after awhile. This DOES NOT mean that the disease has gone away.

4

In women there may be a slight discharge from the vagina with a burning feeling. However, most of the time there are no signs at all. A woman may not realize something is wrong for weeks or months, or even years, after she was infected.

Early in the disease, doctors often can't tell whether a woman is infected.

Tests for gonorrhea have been improved in recent years, but they still aren't 100 per cent reliable. For this reason, many doctors will go ahead and treat a woman if they even suspect that there's a chance she has gonorrhea.

If left untreated, the clap can cause sterility, arthritis, heart trouble and general bad health.

You can catch gonorrhea as many times as you have sex with someone who is infected.

5

SIFF

The first sign of syphilis is usually a sore, which is called a chancre (pronounced shanker). In men it usually appears on the penis; in women it usually occurs inside the vagina.

The chancre, which at first may look like a pimple or wart, soon becomes larger. It doesn't ordinarily hurt or itch. Women usually don't notice it.

If sex contact has been in the mouth or rectum, a sore may develop there.

However, it is possible for the chancre to show up in various parts of the body. It's also possible it won't show up at all.

The chancre will generally appear -- if it's going to -- somewhere between 10 and 90 days after sex contact with a person who has syphilis.

Syphilis left untreated can really ruin your body while you don't even know it.

• The sore goes away in a few weeks. That doesn't mean you are cured.

• You can catch syphilis as many times as you have sex with someone who has it; and you can have syphilis and gonorrhea at the same time.

HERPES VIRUS

(pronounced: *her-pees*

Herpes genitalis is caused by a virus that is usually passed during the sex act. In recent years it has become more and more common -- especially among women.

Groups of painful blisters appear on the sex organs or other areas of sexual contact, but they may also show up on the thighs, buttocks and public area. They soon break open and ooze yellow grey pus. These open sores are big targets for more infection.

Between seven and 28 days after showing up, the blisters go away, but the disease may not go away. They can occur again and again but often with less severe effects.

Women who have had this disease are strongly advised to get a Pap smear on a regular basis and must be alert to its possibility of transmitting the disease to the fetus in case of pregnancy. Sex should be avoided during an outbreak of the disease.

N G U

NGU is an infection of the urinary tract and is the most common sexually transmitted disease in males in the United States.

Signs of NGU are similar to those of gonorrhea. There is a clear or whitish-gray discharge that is thin and mucous-like. Mild to severe burning pain may come with urination.

It is very important to seek medical assistance if these signs appear. NGU is usually treated with tetracycline pills. In some cases gonorrhea and NGU are acquired at the same time, and after the

gonorrhea is cured with penicillin, the NGU symptoms appear. Penicillin is ineffective in curing NGU.

The sexual partner(s) must also be treated because most females and about 22% of males show no signs of NGU.

Left untreated, NGU can lead to prostate problems, infertility, eye problems, skin outbreaks, and/or small ulcers in the mouth. If a female is pregnant, NGU can be fatal to the fetus or can cause serious complications for the baby after birth, including a pneumonia-like illness.

Trichomonas vaginalis is a disease that inflames the vagina. "Trich" germs may be passed during sexual contact or, occasionally, they may be picked up from toilet seats, towels and the like.

Although trich is considered to be a woman's disease, a man can carry the germs and he may get signs of NGU after intercourse with a woman who has trich.

Signs of trich include redness and it-chiness of the vagina, and a smelly, foul discharge.

These signs often go away by themselves, but the disease can still be there. Trichomonas is not considered serious if it is treated promptly, but if it isn't cured it could lead to trouble.

Before going to the doctor, don't douche (wash out the vagina); you may make it difficult for the physician to see what the problem is.

OTHER GENITAL PROBLEMS

Other vaginal disorders

Vaginitis means any noticeable infection of the vagina. Sometimes when doctors don't know what is causing the infection, they call it non-specific vaginitis (NSV). As with NGU in men, NSV in women most often shows up in sexually active females.

Another kind of vaginitis is known as candida albicans, which is a yeast-like fungus. It is not usually transmitted sexually, but it's possible.

You should seek treatment to be sure it isn't gonorrhea and also to stop the infection from traveling up into places like your fallopian tubes (the tubes that connect the ovaries with the uterus).

Crabs-Crab lice are tiny animals that make their home -- by the hundreds -- in the pubic hair (though they travel to other regions). Ordinary soap won't get rid of them. Kwell or Triple X, available from a drugstore, will do the job. Be sure to leave the medication on for the correct amount of time. You don't need to shave the infested area. You can pick up crabs many ways, but sexual contact is the most common way.

Venereal warts-There are various kinds of harmless warts that can appear on the sex organs after sex contact or other close physical contact. Perhaps the most important thing about these warts is that they may not be just warts. Recurring venereal warts in the female may be associated with cervical cancer.

Rubbers (bags, condoms, safes, skins, Trojans, prophylactics) are available without a prescription in drugstores. They are very effective in blocking VD germs from traveling from one partner to another - although they are not 100 per cent safe. The man protects himself from catching it from his partner and he protects his partner from catching it from him.

You can also buy a pro-kit in a drugstore. A pro-kit contains a rubber, as well as ointment which you must apply immediately after intercourse for it to be of any use. This ointment helps to

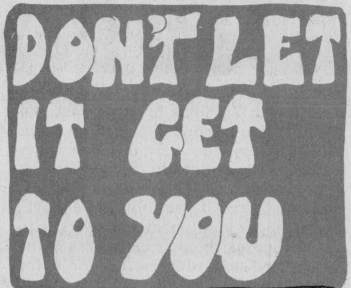

kill VD germs before they start spreading, although it doesn't always work. One kind of ointment is called Sanitube.

It is very helpful to wash with soap and hot water and to urinate immediately after sex -- although it is still possible to get infected. Women may wash out the vagina. However, a woman who is using birth control foam, cream, jelly, or a diaphragm with cream should not douche until six hours after sex, so that the birth control can work.

Of course, the best prevention is not to have sex with someone who might be infected. People who have many sex partners are the ones most likely to catch and spread VD.

ABOUT RUBBERS

A rubber can cost anywhere from 50 cents to $1.00. Some health clinics and Planned Parenthood Centers give out rubbers free. However, in some states there are laws which do not permit minors to buy rubbers, although this is rarely enforced if you look old enough. Even so, we think that teenagers who are having sex should make every effort to get and use rubbers, not only for protection against V.D., but for pregnancy prevention as well.

Girls should not fall for lines boys use, such as "rubbers are too expensive" or "there is no 'feeling' with it." Today's smart woman, won't allow a man in without a rubber, unless she's very sure of him. This goes for women on the pill, too. *The Pill does not prevent V D*

Before Intercourse

Pull the condom over the head of the erect penis (hard on). Leave a 1/2 inch space at the end. (Some condoms already come prepared with this space.)

Slowly unroll until entire penis has been covered.

After Intercourse

Slowly withdraw the penis, holding the end of the condom with the hand to prevent its sliding off.

Use a rubber only once

protect your lover,
wear a rubber

PROTECT YOURSELF

Almost all doctors (private or in clinics) want to treat and cure you, but you may run into a doctor or a nurse from the "old school" who treats you as if you should be punished. There are things you can do. If anyone starts giving you a hard time, humor him or her by agreeing with everything said. Be extra polite. Don't let someone else's meanness stand in the way of your cure.

AND OTHERS

Private doctors treat most of the venereal disease cases, but they report only about 20 per cent to public health authorities. This means that many of the VD cases are not traced for other possible victims.

If you go to a private doctor and find out that you have VD, it may be left up to you to tell anyone you've had sex with. If it is left up to you, protect your partner.

13

IF YOU SUSPECT YOU HAVE IT...

If you think you might have V D , go to your local health center, city venereal disease clinic, or your doctor immediately. The longer you wait, the more damage the disease may be doing. Teenagers in almost all states can be treated without parental knowledge or consent. By law, government health clinics cannot reveal your name when they contact the people you've had sex with.

Venereal disease centers test people for V D without charge. If they find that you have V D , they will provide free treatment (usually penicillin therapy) and contact the people you've had sex with.

Do not try to treat yourself. Treating sores with an ointment containing penicillin only kills the top layers of the germ and leaves the germs underneath alive and spreading.

(14)

WHEN TO SEE A DOCTOR

Since the signs of VD often don't appear, women and men who are sexually active should go for VD testing regularly.

If you have any of the following signs, you should go to a doctor immediately.

Men

• Burning during and shortly after urinating.

• Any sores, warts or pimples on the penis or around it or in any other area of sexual contact.

• Any soreness of the penis.

• Any drip from the penis.

• Any unusual coloring of the urine, such as urine which is reddish or very dark.

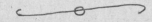

Don't give a dose to the one you love the most.

Women

• Burning while urinating.

• Pain or itchiness in and around the vagina, especially during menstruation.

• Any soreness or redness in and around the sex organ and anus.

• Any sores, warts or pimples in and near the sex organ or other areas of sexual contact.

• A discharge that is yellow, green, or otherwise discolored. (A normal discharge is usually clear or milky.)

• A thick discharge that looks like cottage cheese.

If caught in the early stages, gonorrhea and syphilis can often (but not always) be cured in less than ten days. During this time you should
- Avoid having sex with others until you are cured.
- Avoid masturbating. It can spread the germs to other parts of the body. (Of course, at other times masturbation may be pleasurable and harmless.)
- Not drink any form of alcohol. The alcohol may affect the medicine needed to cure you of VD.
- Tell the people you've had sex with, so they can get treatment.

Important

The cure for VD is not always automatic. This means that after a doctor has treated you, you should have another test a few months later to make sure you were cured.

SOME FUNNY LINES

Here are some lines kids use. Don't be fooled. Protect yourself.

- I may be poor and screw a lot, but I'm clean.
- Don't worry, you can only get V D from a whore.
- Don't worry, I'll pull out before I shoot.
- If you don't want me to shoot, I won't.
- Just for a little while, it takes me a long time before I shoot.

GIMME A BREAK

REMEMBER

- You can be clean, but you may still catch V D
- You can get V D from anyone who has it.
- Withdrawal before a guy comes will not prevent V D (It's not even a good method for birth control.)
- You can get V D from oral sex and intercourse.
- You can get V D from a person of the same or opposite sex.

REALIDAD ACERCA DE LA SÍFILIS Y LA GONORREA

• Las enfermedades venéreas son causadas por gérmenes transmitidos por el contacto sexual.

• La sífilis puede atacar cualquier parte del cuerpo, incluyendo el corazón y el cerebro.

• Si no se cuida la sífilis, puede causar esterilidad, enfermedades cronicas, ceguera, locura y aún la muerte.

• Si una mujer encinta tiene sífilis, puede transmitirla al niño que no ha nacido todavía; así éste será enfermizo, desfigurado o morirá prematuramente.

• Si no se cura la gonorrea, puede causar enfermedades generales, esterilidad, artritis, y enfermidades del corazón.

• El condon (capuchón, goma, gorrito) cuando se usa correctamente, es una buena protección.

• Orinar y lavarse con jabón y agua caliente después del acto sexual puede ayudar.

• Si Usted sabe que una persona está infectada, evite el contacto sexual con aquella persona.

• Cuidado con los primeros síntomas, que son: una illaga en el pene o la vagina para la sífilis; una secreción o sensación inflamatoria para la gonorrea. Recuerde que en la mayoría de las mujeres no hay ningún síntoma durante el primer período de la enfermedad.

• Las enfermedades venéreas se pueden curar. El remedio es facil y efectivo si se las trata pronto.

• Las clínicas locales hacen examenes gratis y dan tambien el tratamiento necesario para curarla.

• El tratamiento y la investigación de las victimas es siempre confidencial.

• La mayoría de los estados tiene leyes que permiten que los adolescentes puedan recibir tratamiento sin el permiso o el conocimiento de los padres.

(18)

BASIC FACTS ABOUT SYPHILIS and GONORRHEA

- Venereal diseases are caused by germs spread by sexual contact.
- Syphilis can attack any part of the body, including the heart and brain.
- Untreated syphilis can cause general bad health, sterility, blindness, insanity and death.
- If a pregnant woman has syphilis she can give it to her unborn baby causing it to be sick, to be deformed, or to die.
- Gonorrhea left untreated can cause general bad health, sterility, arthritis, heart trouble and other serious health problems.
- The rubber, when used right, is good protection.
- Urinating and washing with soap and hot water right after sex may help.
- If you know someone is infected, avoid sex contact with that person.
- Be aware of the first signs, such as a sore on the penis or vagina for syphilis; discharge (drip) and burning feeling for gonorrhea. Remember, though, that most women show no signs during the early stages of infection.
- V D can be cured. Cure is easy and effective if a doctor starts treatment soon after infection.
- Treatment and tracing of V D victims is confidential.
- Most states have laws which allow teenagers to be treated without parental consent or knowledge.

Sex by itself can never make a person more of a man or more of a woman. Womanliness and manliness are measured by a person's integrity and character, not by "going all the way."

0-934978-32-8

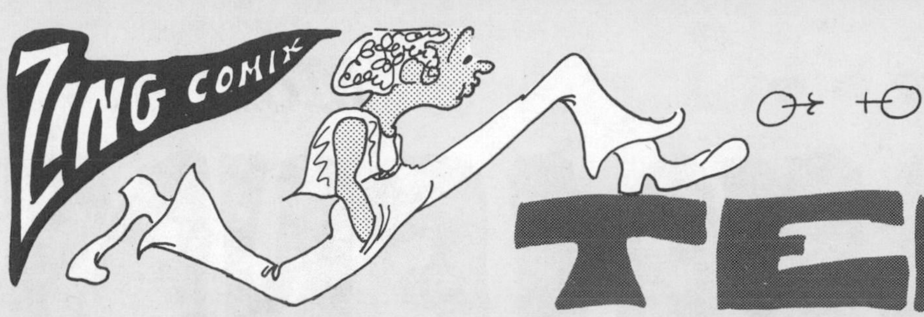

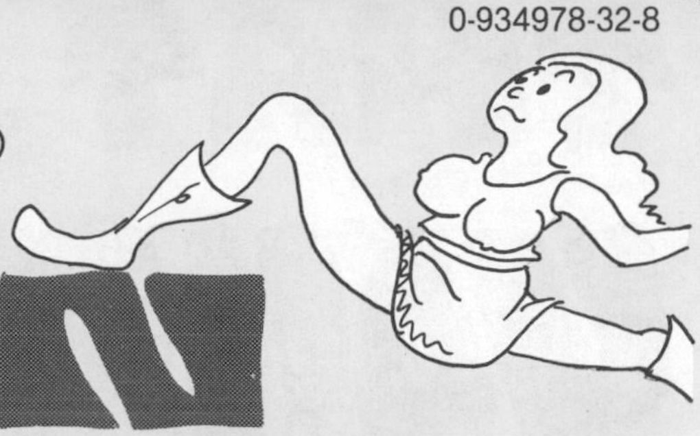

TEN HEAVY FACTS ABOUT SEX THAT

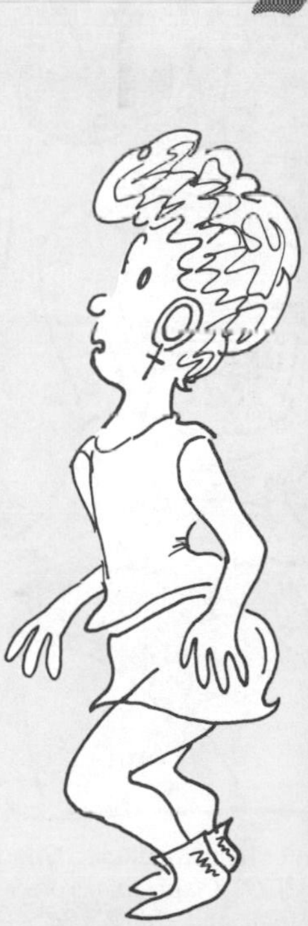

THAT ... Most of YOUR FRIENDS DON'T KNOW

Text: Sol Gordon
Illustration and design: Roger Conant
Facilitator: Kathleen G. Everly

Published by Ed-U Press, Inc.
P.O. Box 583
Fayetteville, N.Y. 13066

Other titles in this series of educational comic books include: *How Can You Tell If You're Really in Love?*, *V.D. Claptrap*, *Protect Yourself From Becoming an Unwanted Parent* and *Juice Use — Special Hangover Edition*. These booklets and *Heavy Facts* are available for $1.95 each from Ed-U Press. Bulk rates available.

Revised 1987 ©1971, by Ed-U Press, Inc.

YOUR PARENTS DIDN'T TELL YOU

1 SEX THOUGHTS

A PENNY FOR YOUR THOUGHTS

COST YOU A FIVER FOR MY THOUGHTS... THEY'RE X-RATED

Sexual thoughts -- no matter how weird -- that pop into your mind cannot harm you as long as you don't worry about them.

But, if your fantasies (sexual or otherwise) make you feel guilty, you probably won't be able to avoid having them. If you know that it is usual to get all sorts of way-out thoughts, then the thoughts you don't like will occur less and less.

However, if your religion teaches that it is immoral for you to *deliberately* draw out sexual or aggressive fantasies, that is your business -- so long as it is something you control. But it is not sensible to get into a guilty, panicky sweat about a thought or image that you don't really want or enjoy, or that just occurs to you.

Remember: There is a big difference between having some thoughts of doing something wrong and actually making up your mind to do the wrong thing.

2 MASTURBATION

Masturbation is a form of sexual release for most males and females. You won't injure your body by masturbating -- no matter how often.

If masturbation has become a habit that makes you feel guilty, it is more like self-punishment than self-enjoyment. Just about the only way to break a strong habit is to somehow manage to put up with the tension that results when you don't do *it* (masturbate,

smoke, overeat, or whatever). The tension will decrease as you get used to the change.

Many people of all ages get pleasure from masturbating. Still, if you have religious or moral objections, then don't do it. A person doesn't have to masturbate in order to be sexually healthy.

Remember too -- "wet dreams" (the release of semen during a sexual dream) are perfectly normal and happen to almost all boys.

 HOMOSEXUAL

Most people, men and women, have occasional thoughts about homosexual acts, and many people have had homosexual experiences. This doesn't make them homosexuals.

A gay or lesbian is a person who, in adult life, has sex relations with members of the same sex.

Homosexuality is not a sickness or inherited. A few homosexual experiences won't make you homosexual if you don't choose to be. Letting yourself be bothered by fear of homosexuality in yourself or others doesn't make sense.

Most people are heterosexual. Some people are homosexual or bi-sexual. A few adults choose not to have sexual relations -- which is okay, too. We have no right to condemn a person because of his or her sexual orientation.

Any type of sexual behavior can be considered "abnormal" when it is compulsive and exploitative (using people without caring much about their well-being). That's when sex is an expression of a problem rather than an enrichment of a relationship.

HEALTH ALERT

Due to the AIDS crisis, anal and oral sex are not considered safe, especially for homosexuals, bisexuals and their partners. Anal and vaginal intercourse and oral sex should be avoided by heterosexuals who are unsure of the fidelity of their sexual partners or whose partners are intravenous drug users.

'PERVERSIONS'

A lot of people wonder about oral and anal sex (mouth to penis, vagina or anus; or penis to anus). Some say that such acts are unacceptable and degrading. Other people consider them to be a normal part of making out or a substitute for intercourse.

We say, no one has the right to condemn a person on the basis of that person's manner of sexual expression.*

If this, or any other, form of sexual activity goes against your religious beliefs, don't do it.

*Obviously, if one person *forces* another to engage in any sexual act, or if an adult has sex with a child, that is not good.

5 VD

Venereal disease (VD) is spread by having sexual contact (heterosexual or homosexual) with someone who has it. In fact, most people now refer to venereal diseases as STD (Sexually Transmitted Diseases). Besides intercourse, VD spreads through oral and anal sex (even open-mouthed kissing).

A fairly good way to cut down chances of getting VD is to urinate and wash your genitals with soap and hot water before and right after sex relations. This, however, is *no guarantee* against VD. (Women using contraceptive foam should not douche until six hours after relations.)

The two most serious forms of VD are gonorrhea and syphilis. First signs of gonorrhea are pus and "burning" while urinating. The first sign of syphilis is a sore on the penis, or in the vagina, mouth or rectum. Women may not notice any signs when they have VD.

More and more women are becoming sterile (unable to have children) because of untreated VD.

Signs of VD go away by themselves without medical treatment. But the disease can still be doing damage. You just don't know you have it.

Watch out for herpes because that's not curable. For more information, call the toll free VD Hotline (1-800-227-8922).

You cannot be cured without treatment from a doctor. Most states have sensibly revised their laws to permit teenagers to be examined and treated without parental consent or knowledge.

The County Health Clinic is usually the best place to go. Or you can call on your local hotline, free clinic or Planned Parenthood.

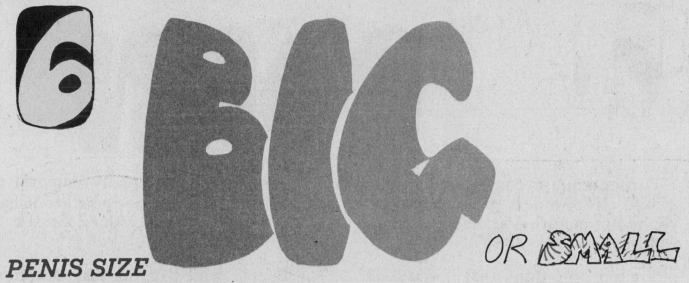

6 BIG OR SMALL

PENIS SIZE

Boys often wonder about the size of their penis and girls help them worry by making remarks. But no matter how big or small, the sexual pleasure -- for either sex -- is not determined by penis size.

Besides, you can't tell the size of a penis by looking at it when it is not erect. Some penises that look small actually become bigger when erect (erections are sometimes called hardons or boners) than those that look big when not erect.

BREAST SIZE

Many girls are concerned about whether their breasts are too small or too big, and boys who make comments don't help matters. Breast size is not a sign of your sexuality. Mature people appreciate and value people for being themselves rather than for what they look like.

Also, during the teen years, a girl's breasts can grow at different rates. This is normal.

 **PORN**

Pornography becomes boring after awhile. If porno is your main bag, you're not mature -- sexually or otherwise.

Some people think that if you look at pictures of nudes or read descriptions of sex acts, you might become corrupted. What is really immoral is deliberate deception -- whether it has to do with politics, values, or sex.

People with a good sex education usually don't have a big interest in pornography.

8

WHEN CAN A GIRL GET PREGNANT?

There is no 100 per cent safe time when a girl can have intercourse without risking pregnancy. But, in general, most girls are not able to get pregnant during menstruation or in the two or three days after menstruation.

A girl can get pregnant the first time she has sexual intercourse. She can get pregnant if she has sex standing up, sitting down, or in any other position.

Two ways of avoiding unwanted pregnancy: self control or birth control.

9 BIRTH CONTROL
-PILLS & RUBBERS-

The Pill -- still the most effective. Take heed: just taking one or two is no help. Females must take their pills regularly under a doctor's care. (The Pill has not yet been proved safe for adolescents who are in the early stages of their physical development.)

Other medical birth controls are the IUD (intrauterine device) and the diaphragm.

The best birth control available without a prescription is a combina-

tion of the rubber for the man and the foam (which is inserted before sex) for the woman. When buying rubbers, ask for a package of condoms. Females be sure to get contraceptive foam. Both are available in drugstores.

Douching (washing out the vagina) -- no matter with what -- and the rhythm method are not trustworthy ways to prevent pregnancy. The same goes for withdrawal of the penis before "coming" (ejaculation) -- although this is better than no protection at all.

GALOSHES?

WARNING: The Pill does not prevent V.D. If you have intercourse with someone who has V.D. and he does not use a condom, your chances of getting it are greater if you are on the Pill.

Having a medical abortion during the early weeks of pregnancy is less risky than giving birth. However, *abortion is very dangerous when not done by a physician.*

Medical abortions are now legal in all states during the first 12 weeks of pregnancy. During the second three months a state may restrict abortions somewhat. (For example, between the 12th and 16th week routine abortion is not wise because of the possibility of injury to the uterus.) During the final 10 weeks of pregnancy, when chances of live birth are high, a state may outlaw abortion, except if the woman's life is in danger.

Once a woman has faced the moral issues involved in an abortion, no one has the right to require that she have or not have one. She

must decide, on her own responsibility, whether abortion in her case is right or wrong.

As soon as a woman discovers that she is pregnant, she should get professional care. Teenagers who are afraid to get help because parents might get upset should seek counseling at a local Planned Parenthood or at a county or hospital family planning clinic. They can help you prepare for a baby or arrange an abortion, or help you make plans for adoption. (Of course, it is still a good idea to communicate with your parents about your pregnancy, even though it may cause tension.)

You may run into a few cold people who act as if you should be punished. Don't let such insensitivity influence you -- one way or the other. Teenagers are entitled by law to confidential treatment.

VIRGIN RIGHTS

Males and females have a right to be virgins. These days there is a lot of pressure on guys to "prove" their masculinity by having sex and there is increasing pressure for girls to "get with it" and screw.

People who choose to be virgins should stick to their guns. Those who make fun of virgins reveal their own sexual insecurity. On the other hand, some boys who fool around themselves say they want to marry a virgin. We say, we hope you'll marry a person, not a hymen.

SEX PROBLEMS

If it turns out that your first few sexual experiences weren't enjoyable or satisfactory, don't assume that there is anything wrong with you. A lot of people have temporary difficulties when they first begin.

For example, some men find that they are impotent -- unable to have an erection when they want to have intercourse -- or that they have premature ejaculation -- coming before or im-mediately after the penis enters the vagina.

Some women don't have orgasms. They don't enjoy sex, or even if they do, they worry because they don't get an orgasm. (It is not necessary to have orgasm to enjoy sex.)

Such difficulties are usually solved in time when two people work at their problems with sympathy and under-standing for each other. If problems persist, seek professional help.

READY?

- Are you mature?

- Are you in love?

- Are you old enough to handle possible consequences by yourself?

- Are both of you ready for a baby or, if you aren't

- Are you using birth control?

- What about marriage?

Don't fall for lines like:
   If you really love me, you'll have sex with me.

Reply:
   If you really loved me, you wouldn't put this kind of pressure on me.

OR NOT?

- **Are you less interested in the health and well-being of the other person than in satisfying your own needs?**

- **Do you use sex mostly as a way of trying to "prove" that you are somebody?**

- **Do you have sex a lot when you really don't want to, getting very little pleasure out of it?**

MORALITY IS GOOD FOR YOU

FOR GUYS:

- No sex unless you are ready for it.
- Protect your lover; wear a rubber.
- Don't reveal your sexual inadequacy by boasting about your sexploits.
- Don't go around hurting girls because you feel insecure. (A guy who is always on the make basically hates women.)
- *Machismo* is when you're man enough to share responsibility for a pregnancy.
- No sex with anyone you don't care about or who doesn't really care about you.

FOR GIRLS:

- No sex unless you are ready for it. (Don't fall for lines like: "If you don't have sex with me, we might as well stop seeing each other.")

- No sex with a guy without a reliable method of birth control. (If the guy is too cheap to spend 35 cents for a condom, he shouldn't be allowed in.)

- No sex with anyone you don't care about or who doesn't really care about you. (Find out if he'll go out with you even if you won't have sex with him.)

- Support Women's Liberation NOW!

FOR REAL
People who feel good about themselves don't go around hurting other people.

REMEMBER
Sex is never a test of love.

IF YOU WANT TO KNOW MORE:
Facts About Sex For Today's Youth
Sol Gordon

When Living Hurts
Sol Gordon

The Teenage Survival Book
Sol Gordon

Available from Ed-U Press, P.O. Box 583, Fayetteville, NY 13066

RELATIONSHIPS

Relationships
>   born out of desperation
>   seldom
>   last
longer than relationships
>   fashioned out of despair
Relationships
>   kindled by needs
are rarely fired by humor or desire

If I need you
>   (for some reason or other)
Or if you need me
>   (et cetera)
It often becomes a mismatch of
>   different
>   changing
>   faltering
>   disintegrating
emotions
But if we want
>   *each other*
We stand a chance
because people who want each other
>   leave room for
>   disappointments
>   privacy and
>   peak periods of passion.

EVEN LOVE

Really meaningful experiences in life
have peaks
    of brief duration
which are repeatable
    Even love
    is
    imperfect
leaves us open
    to be
        hurt
        vulnerable
        misunderstood
Yet
leaves room for
    growth
    excitement
    joy
becoming more ourselves
    by offering more to the other
but that doesn't mean
    that our timing is always right
even when we love each other

NOT YET MET

We
knew
the farewell
could not spoil our volatile love
fashioned
when each of us
too vulnerable for imprinting to fail

Now at last
the reunion (in the offing)
can only
underestimate
a reality
grown older
wiser?

for
quiet love
and laughs remembered
with passion
still to come
in happy embrace
of a future
not yet
(never to be?)
exorcised

LOVE CAN AFFORD TO BE BLIND ONLY ON THE FIRST DAY OF IT

Our brief encounters
that one day by chance
touched me more
than instant intimacy
the night before
with someone
more enthusiastic.

Our unscheduled interludes
rising and descending
in meaning and intensity
thrusting close to love
failed to inspire trust
(I'm glad to say)
left you afraid, excited, worried
before risking anything
you would regret.

Why did you happen to be
so dear to me?

Who needs you anyway?
There is always someone else
(I'm not insecure)
I can get along without you
to be sure
But why should I?
Should I?

NO ONE KNOWS

Does one ever
  recapture
a flight of fancy
a past passion
a lost regret

Can one ever
fall in love
in retrospect

The present fire
offers a warm flow

The past fire
a bittersweet memory

There is always hope?

REJECTED BY GLIDE IN SAN FRANCISCO

Even after lunch at Salmagundi's, sight shopping at Gump's,
chatting with the street people handicrafters,
gaping at the new St. Mary's Cathedral and the ultra Embarcadero,
topping the Mark, cable carring about,
the Cannery and Ghiradelli Square, the Palace of the Legion of Honor,
the Experience in the Queen of American cities still is
attending a Sunday morning service at the
Glide Memorial United Methodist Church with Cecil Williams preachin'.
Now everybody is welcome at this church and that's a fact—
even if you are not sure Mary was a virgin.
So, after the singing and the clapping and the loud, electrifying music
and a sermon to end all sermons with Cecil announcing
that he was pregnant (everybody seemed to understand)
it ends.
And then everyone joins hands or puts their arms around each other
and sings the parting song of siblinghood
But the person next to me moved away from me and
embraced someone far away. I felt rejected by the entire Glide Church.
That's like being thrown out of *The Last Whole Earth Catalog* (Revised).
Instead of reaching out to someone else
I fled.
It took all of an hour and a mushy ice-cream sundae for me to recover.
Then I remembered Cecil's prophecy.
"You are the ANSWER," he said.
So I went about all day seeking the QUESTION. I kept asking people
"Where are you going?"
and if they wanted to find out, I asked the question
"WHAT ARE YOU waiting for?"
I felt marvelous.
Thank you Cecil.
for giving back my time (has come).

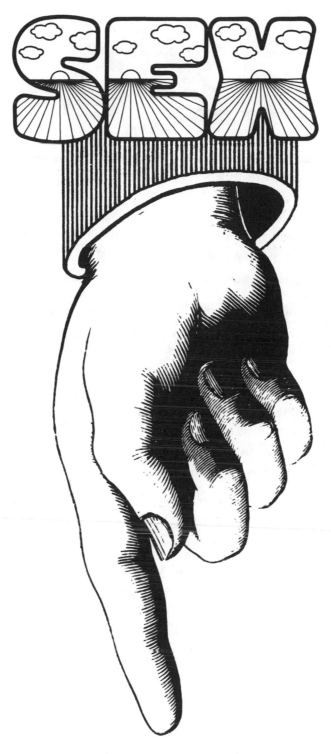

is a good thing, and important.

It looms very large and menacing in a life that is empty and frustrating.

It is an exquisite part of a life that is developing, searching, and striving for harmony.

93

Here are a few thoughts about sex that we feel could be helpful to young people who are still into life:

If you don't feel like reading much

but still want to know more than you do (maybe), turn immediately to the comic books. You can always come back to this section later.

will the real sexual revolution stand up!

People have become so performance-oriented, so preoccupied with the number of times they've scored, with orgasms, and with positions, that they avoid intimacy and become sexual acrobats or, more likely, bored with life itself.

Who knows what this revolution means anymore? Except that:

 **One in four pregnancies is still unwanted.
The birth rate is going down in every age group
except among teenagers.**

Some 600,000 adolescent girls gave birth to mostly unplanned, unwanted children in 1990. About half married to "cover" the pregnancy.

 **There were also more than three million new cases of
V.D. (now also called STD—Sexually Transmitted
Diseases) in 1990.**

Our studies reveal that young people are having sex earlier and more frequently than in the past. Also, the younger they have sex, the less they know about it. We have also found that the average teenager must pretend (at least in public) that he or she knows everything there is to know about sex.

It's really odd how a lot of people think the reason so many girls are sexually active these days is because of the availability of contraception. Yet research has shown that only about 20% of teenage couples use effective birth control each time they have sex.

IS BED-ED DEAD?

You can rarely rely on schools or even colleges for an adequate sex education. If they give a course at all it usually deals with "plumbing." It turns out to be a relentless pursuit of the fallopian tubes.

In one school the high school gym teacher introduced his *course* to a segregated male audience like this: "Hey fellas, that *thing* between your legs is not a muscle, don't exercise it."

In another school the students complained that the teacher taught sex so clean it came out dirty.

The following letter appeared in a New Jersey high school newspaper:

To the Editor:

As a male who has finally attained the privilege to learn about sex, I am most disappointed. I thought that senior sex education would provide the answers to my sexual hang-ups. Instead, I learn that the prostate (?) gland is underneath the bladder and above the testicle, and that a woman's larynx is smaller than a man's. In addition, a certain film left me with the impression that holding hands leads to pregnancies. I won't argue with the importance of this information, but how is it relevant to sex education? What happens when the teacher refuses to call "sexual intercourse" sexual intercourse and refers to it as, "it" or "that", and other indefinite pronouns? We do not lack the maturity to discuss the various aspects of sex (love, perversions, marriage, morals, etc.), so why are these topics avoided? Perhaps an improvement in the subject matter taught might awaken the growing number of boys to whom the term "bed-ed" has come to mean just that — a period of sleep.

95

SEX, READY OR NOT!

Most young people will have had sexual intercourse several or many times during their adolescence. When young people have sex they don't ask their parents' consent. They simply know that their parents will say no. Teenagers also don't ask me or any other counselors, because we all have a tendency to say "no!" But who's listening? So, I quickly add, "Look, if you are not going to pay attention to me, at least use birth control."

The main problem is that *most* young people experimenting with their first intercourse do not use birth control. Many girls think it is not romantic to be prepared. Irresponsible boys feel it's the girl's job to worry about birth control. Some girls fall for lines like, "Don't worry about it, I'll pull out in time," or, "I don't get any feeling when I use a rubber (condom)" or, "It's too expensive." Girls should respond, "What about my feelings when I'm pregnant, need an abortion, or give birth?" or, "All the boys I know enjoy it with a condom on. What's wrong with you?" Or even your own line.

There are other problems when young, immature people have sex. The first experiences, often due to unfortunate circumstances and/or lack of knowledge, tend to be disappointing or without pleasure and are frequently misinterpreted by the people involved to mean that there must be something wrong with them.

Many adults who have consulted me because of sexual problems have been able to trace them to bad sexual experiences they had as teenagers. Of course, many people can also recall that their only good love and sexual experiences took place in their teen years.

So the best I can say to young people is that if you want sex, it's better to wait at least until you are older (in college or working) but if you are going to anyway, use birth control and join the campaign against absurd state laws that prohibit teenagers from getting birth control information and services without parental consent.

VIRGINS HAVE RIGHTS TOO!

SOMETIMES A YOUNG MAN WILL SAY TO ME, "I WANT TO MARRY A VIRGIN."

I REPLY, "I HOPE YOU'LL MARRY A PERSON, NOT A HYMEN."

It is safe to assume that if about 70% of females who marry have sex before marriage, then about 30% wait until marriage. And notwithstanding the figure for males who wait (about 20%) we must emphatically declare that virgins have rights too even if they are a minority.

Despite "official" support for virgins, this group is rapidly becoming more ridiculed and more vulnerable.

96

And because everybody who is anybody supports virgins, there are no "pressures" for virgins to organize to protect their rights. Can you imagine an organization called the Virgin Activist League with the slogan "Power to the Virgins" and a button declaring "Virginity Is Beautiful"?

Now, I happen to believe that committed virgins should stick to their guns and not be intimidated by peer pressure. Just because some of the worst elements in the Establishment support (often for people other than themselves) the virginal state is no reason to question its validity. Some of society's best people also support virginity. Our society, for its very survival, needs more people who have the courage of their convictions.

It is no accident that in my 25 years as a psychologist no young person has ever asked my consent for sex. Yet I am frequently asked if it is normal to wait until marriage. I, of course, reply "yes." I could be very sanctimonious and stop there, but I add: "If you are going to wait, I trust that you won't expect simultaneous orgasms on your wedding night. Otherwise you might ask yourself the question 'For this I waited?' " ("For this I waited?" is an effective comment only with a Jewish accent.)

SEXUAL ORIENTATION

It is no longer believed that homosexuality is caused by any one thing or special combination of factors. Homosexuals exist in every culture and society. The ancient Greek culture found homosexuality acceptable; our culture has frowned upon it.

Homosexuality is not hereditary, biological, chemical, or constitutional. I suspect that few people would be exclusively one way or another if we were more open about our sexual attractions. As an example, men in our society are especially frightened by normal desires for intimacy with other males because of their fear of being diagnosed as homosexual.

In any case, we now know that homosexual experiences are not rare during childhood and adolescence. These experiences do not necessarily mean that a person will embrace a gay life-style as an adult. One (and even some) homosexual experience doesn't make a person homosexual any more than one (or some) heterosexual experience makes a person heterosexual, any more than one (or some) drink makes a person an alcoholic.

It is completely untrue that if you have homosexual thoughts or dreams you must be a homosexual. Mature people are aware that they have both homosexual and heterosexual feelings, even though the majority of them

97

prefer sexual activities with members of the opposite sex. In this connection you should know that it is not easy to judge whether a person is a homosexual. Some feminine-looking men or masculine-looking women are heterosexual, and some highly "masculine," muscular, "all-American" types of men are homosexual.

There is no such thing as latent homosexuality in the sense that it is, by itself, a problem. Everyone starts out with latent bi-, homo-, auto-, and hetero-sexualities. People who are afraid of their healthy sexual impulses have a problem no matter what expression it takes.

The gay liberation movement has made it abundantly clear that homosexuals are, in fact, just as healthy or unhealthy as heterosexuals. Sexual preference does not determine whether a person is mature or "normal."

Risking rejection is also risking acceptance.

I hope there will come a time when people's sexual preferences will be of little or no interest to lawmakers and certainly none of anybody's business (unless that body is an unwilling partner).

Being "with it" doesn't mean you have to like anal, oral, auto, homo or group sexuality. But having fixed, powerful emotions like "revolting," "disgusting," "perverse," "obscene," or "unnatural" in response to behavior that is enjoyable *to others* often means *you* have a problem. It's especially serious when you make a big deal out of your aversion. For example, we occasionally hear men say, "If any faggot so much as comes near me, I'll kill him."

A heterosexual person can respond to a homosexual advance by saying (or feeling): "That's your preference, but it's not mine." A homosexual can say the same thing to a heterosexual.

Fig. 40   *Fig. 41*   *Fig. 42*

Other responses could be (not necessarily verbal):

**I have a headache.
Not this time.
I'm faithful to my partner.
You are not attractive to me.
I'm not promiscuous.
I'm straight/gay.
I'll try it and see what it is like.
It's that time of the month.
No, thank you.**

Or, just walk away.

sexual arousal

Popular culture, especially the mass media, creates the notion that there are standard ways to get aroused. Men, for example, are "supposed" to be aroused by the pretty girl selling automobiles or by Playboy's bunnies. That's all right except that men who aren't aroused by the current fashion often feel compelled to fake it. The fact is that human beings are sexually aroused by an endless variety of stimuli.

And *not* knowing that *all* forms of arousal are all right is what causes trouble. The problem is somewhat more acute with men only because they sometimes can't hide obvious hard-ons. But men who are comfortable with their sexuality (in this case, who don't feel guilty about getting a hard-on) should be able to get rid of an erection about as easily as they can get one.

Some people feel guilty if they are sexually aroused when playing with children, roughing it with dogs, being attracted to their parents, sitting in moving vehicles, having sadistic fantasies, looking at pornography. If you can accept the arousal experience without guilt, no harm is done. And why not enjoy some of it? The only real problem occurs if you can get excited only by thoughts or acts you or your partner find unacceptable and exploitative.

DO YOUR SEXUAL THOUGHTS BOTHER YOU?

Sexual thoughts, wishes, dreams, and daydreams are normal, no matter how far out. *Behavior* is what counts the most. Thoughts, images, and fantasies cannot, in themselves, hurt you or others. If your religion teaches that deliberately cultivating sexual or sadistic fantasies is immoral, that's your business, so long as it is something you can control. But to get hung up because of passing thoughts that you have little control over is not only pointless, it may even be harmful.

Guilt is the energy for the repetition of fantasies that are unacceptable to you. The people who massively repress their fantasies or become preoccupied with them because of guilt are the ones most likely to harm themselves and others.

AN EXAMPLE

A 15-year-old boy caught a glimpse of his 13-year-old sister taking a shower. The first thing that came into his mind was to have sex with her. He felt terribly guilty and could not free his mind from the image or the sexual wish. Nobody in his family could understand why he began to avoid his friends, became hostile to his sister and seemed to be getting more and more depressed.

Here, of course, guilt caused the sex fantasy to return over and over again. It became an obsession (involuntary repetition of ideas) and he was preoccupied with it. After a while he might "forget" (repress) the incident and only hostility to the sister would remain. What a pity that this boy didn't understand that his wish was normal. Had he known it, the thought would have remained with him for a brief time (whether he enjoyed it or not doesn't matter) and nothing would have happened.

Anybody with even the slightest bit of imagination has, from time to time, murderous, sadistic, incestuous, or rape fantasies. That does not mean they are going to act them out. As a matter of fact, accepting as normal one's "unacceptable" thoughts is the best way to keep them under voluntary control.

"Close your eyes, Jeffy — I'm comin' in."

Fantasies

● It is common for people to have sexual thoughts when they are masturbating, having sexual intercourse, when they are daydreaming and at other, sometimes less convenient, times.

● No matter what you think about (even having sex with someone other than the person you are having it with), it's best when it is enjoyable. It's even all right if it's not enjoyable, provided you don't feel guilty.

● Almost all reasonably healthy people *at times* find their fantasies more exciting than the real thing.

AUTO-EROTIC

Nearly everyone these days says that masturbation is all right . . . a normal developmental stage (and then there is a pause) . . . "It's all right if you don't do it too much."

And nearly everyone is asking the question "How much is too much?" Once a year? Twice a month? After every meal?

The answer: Once is too much if you don't enjoy it.

In my day, it was simple. No question about it. From playing with yourself you got acne, tired blood, insanity and blindness (that's why I wear glasses). We were pioneers in those days!

Funny now—sad once

Those days weren't as far back as you might think. But even further back, this is the kind of advice kids were given. It's from *Safe Counsel* (Practical Advice About Sex, Sin and Sane Living), first published in 1873 and revised by Intext Press in 1973.

"There are some boys who are so strong that they can go on for some time, even two or three years, and do not show serious damage. There are others who give evidence of their loss of virility immediately and finally break in a pitiful way, but in general we are safe in saying that one or more of these results will follow the practice of self-abuse . . . retarded development of the body . . . another mark of the damage done by this secret habit is the weariness of the boy . . . another result of the abuse of the body is the weakening of the nerves . . . The discharge of the semen in the final act of self abuse is a severe strain for it brings with it the arousing of the whole body and ends in a considerable shock . . . Going along with the mental and physical damage is also the moral loss which comes from this habit."

Masturbation is a normal sexual expression for all people, no matter at what age or stage in life you happen to be—a child, teenager, young adult, middle-aged, elderly—and whether you are single or married.

Compulsive eating, talking, sleeping, or masturbating is an example of natural behavior that can indicate problems. This does not making eating, talking, sleeping, or masturbating unnatural. If I had to settle for one compulsive behavior to express my problems I would certainly select masturbation.

A lot of men and women don't often admit it, but they achieve their best orgasms by masturbating. A lot of married people with satisfactory sex lives masturbate. Some people (not many) masturbate hardly at all or not at all. That's all right too. Guilt about masturbation is about the only thing that's bad about it.

"IF I AM NOT FOR MYSELF,
WHO WILL BE FOR ME?
AND IF I AM ONLY FOR MYSELF,
WHAT AM I
AND IF NOT NOW, WHEN?"
—HILLEL

Want to know more about this stuff?

Read:

Personal Issues in Human Sexuality: A Guidebook for Better Sexual Health, by Sol Gordon and Craig W. Snyder (Allyn & Bacon, 1989)
Why Love Is Not Enough, by Sol Gordon (Bob Adams, 1990)

Whom to See for Help

(For Nonsexual Problems as Well)

The best places to try first for information are hotlines; free clinics; Planned Parenthood; a professional, or a clinic associated with the American Association of Marriage and Family Counselors, Rational Emotive Therapists, Masters and Johnson clinics; humanistic psychologists. Don't remain with any professional who you feel after the first couple of sessions is not competent and really does not care about you. Remember the professional is your employee—you can fire her/him anytime. Don't be intimidated by credentials or affluence. The professionals to be on guard against are those who start out by saying that therapy is going to take a long time (years). There is no evidence that sexual problems need take a long time to cure or that analysts or psychiatrists are any better at it than clergymen or social workers. This is *not to say*, however, that for some people therapy should not continue for a long period—even years.

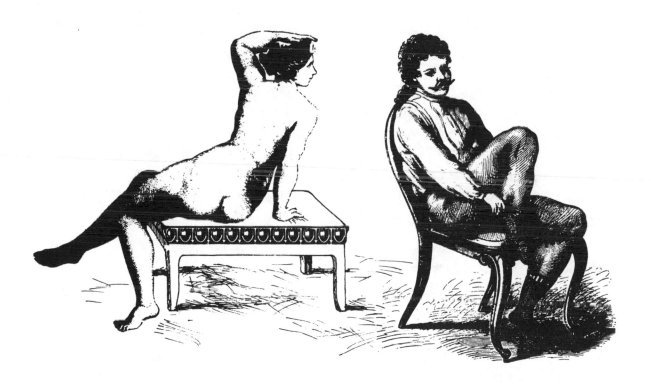

If you want a little distance from someone you are supposed to be close to, be polite.

TOWARD A PSYCHOLOGY OF BEING SEXUALLY VERY HEALTHY*

To achieve healthy sexual adjustment, I believe
we must seek these basic freedoms:

FREEDOM *from sexual stereotyping*

Cultural definitions of masculinity and femininity are the key to sexual stereotyping. Our culture has insisted on the idea that men should be aggressive, worldly, strong, rational, and dominant, and that women should be passive, domestic, weak, emotional, and submissive. The destruction of these stereotypes is necessary to achieve honest human relationships.

We have also been led to believe that heterosexual love is the only legitimate and normal kind of love. We must recognize that homosexuality (whether male or female) and bisexuality are also valid sexual behaviors. We must also guarantee the right to reveal or not to reveal sexual interests and tendencies.

Furthermore, we have to break out of stereotypes, new and old, about marriages and living together, and recognize *both* as healthy arrangements for two people who respect and care about each other. Other stereotypes that need to be legitimized are such unconventional pairings as an older woman with a younger man, elderly couples, interracial couples, and couples who decide not to have children. We must also eliminate discrimination against people who choose to be single and/or celibate.

FREEDOM *from sexual oppression*

The exploitation of women for the purpose of selling products and services reduces all women to sexual objects and creates narrow, stereotypical standards of beauty. Women are also exploited as workers, being underpaid for most jobs, and receive little recognition—and, usually, no pay—for being housewives and mothers. People must be made aware of this exploitation on all levels—economic, educational, social, and sexual—before any two people can relate with sexual honesty.

Men are also exploited because of roles they are supposed to play in our society. For example, men who are not interested in sports, or who like

*A manifesto developed by the author and several of his students at Syracuse University

housekeeping, are ridiculed and often are deprived of economic opportunities because they do not fit into a company's image of what constitutes the male role.

Women, too, exploit men and expect them to fulfill roles such as "provider," "daddy," or "stud."

FREEDOM *of information*

Access to basic information must be guaranteed to all regardless of age, sex, or intelligence. In the case of mentally handicapped people, special efforts must be made to give them the information they need in a way they can understand. Freedom of information should also include the right to read literature that has been subject to societal restrictions. Only complete freedom of information can ensure an educated and enlightened populace.

FREEDOM *from repression of the last generation*

Young people must realize that many parents do not have adequate information about sexual behavior, or if they do, they are often unable or unwilling to communicate it to their children. Even parents who present the basic facts may find it difficult to deal with their child's feelings about his or her own emerging sexuality. Perhaps because of their own fears and misconceptions, many parents overreact to their children's questions or sexual behavior. Although parents are a good source for moral values and attitudes, we must recognize the possibility of their passing on misinformation, prejudices, and personal problems concerning sexual matters. What is needed as much as school programs is a massive sex education program directed at parents and newlyweds. Our feelings and knowledge about sex become exceedingly important when we realize that we may pass on unhealthy attitudes to *our* children.

FREEDOM *from research nonsense and sex myths*

Access to accurate information is crucial to a healthy sexuality. Unfortunately, not everything in print is reliable information. One "study" reported that males were "in their prime" at age 17, and females in their late twenties. Popular reports like these, and even more reputable studies, often confuse people seeking a commonsense approach to sexuality. Some research is extremely valuable for debunking sexual myths (for example, some of the work of Masters and Johnson). However, a flood of popular articles on sex in magazines and newspapers actually creates new myths. We must find a sane perspective based on common sense and the basic facts about sexual behavior.

105

FREEDOM *to control one's own body*

We must be free from legal controls of our own bodies. This freedom would prohibit legislation restricting medical abortion, voluntary sterilization, consensual sexual relations among adults, contraceptive information and devices for minors, and privacy of sexual expression. Also implied would be the right to choose one's own life-style and sexual partners. Inherent, too, is the right to proper medical care and access to contraceptive devices for anyone who wants them.

FREEDOM *to express affection*

Until we overcome our fear of expressing our affection for one another, regardless of gender, we cannot achieve full sexual adjustment. Our culture now suffers great anxiety about even *touching* another person (hugging, holding hands, etc.). We must be able to feel free to touch other people, even a member of the same sex, without fear of critical diagnosis and fixation. This is especially important with children, who want and enjoy physical affection from adults and peers.

FREEDOM *of sexual expression for the handicapped*

We must recognize and facilitate sexual expression among the mentally retarded, emotionally disturbed, and physically handicapped. Special educational efforts should be directed to helping these people find appropriate sexual opportunities.

    While these freedoms are a necessary precondition for healthy sexuality, they are not without their corollary responsibilities. These moral or ethical standards also must be commonly accepted.

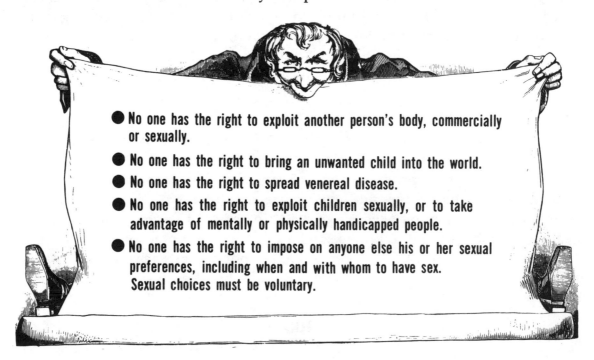

- No one has the right to exploit another person's body, commercially or sexually.
- No one has the right to bring an unwanted child into the world.
- No one has the right to spread venereal disease.
- No one has the right to exploit children sexually, or to take advantage of mentally or physically handicapped people.
- No one has the right to impose on anyone else his or her sexual preferences, including when and with whom to have sex. Sexual choices must be voluntary.

These freedoms and responsibilities cannot be guaranteed by the Constitution but will evolve gradually as people's consciousness about sexuality changes. The most important factors in effecting this change will be a willingness to communicate openly and to explore our preconceived notions about sexuality. Complete access to information will make the process of change easier.

Eventually we will come to realize that any two adults have the right to voluntary nonexploitative sexual relations. Ideally, their relationship should lead to and enhance each other's personal growth.

THE HEART OF THE MATTER

Sex without intimacy is, or rapidly becomes,
a drag
despite the bragging and lies, and the
proclamations of pseudo prophets; the
sexual revolution offers little comfort
to millions of lonely, alienated people
needing love but getting laid* instead

WHAT'S MISSING?

What's missing is the fun and joy of sexuality that is shared with a person you love. It's not included because that part is up to you.

*An archaic term for having sex without intimacy

U S A

United to Save America *from*

- **The John Birch Society**
- **American Nazi Party**
- **Censorship**
- **Ku Klux Klan**
- **Book Burners**
- **Violations of the First Amendment**

- **Citizens for Excellence in Education**
- **The So-Called Moral Majority**
- **Compulsory Pregnancy Zealots**
- **Bible Bigots**
- **Eagle Forum**
- **American Family Association**

United to Save America *for*

Democracy
Freedom of Speech
Press
Assembly
Religious
Worship
and "Choice"

December 15th is National Bill of Rights Day

The Heart of the Matter:

Congress shall make no law respecting an establishment of religion, or prohibiting the free exercise thereof; or abridging the freedom of speech, or of the press; or the right of the people peaceably to assemble and to petition the government for a redress of grievances.

First Amendment to the Bill of Rights of the U.S. Constitution — passed December 15th, 1791

The women's liberation movement is also the best single force for the liberation of men. While women have suffered the most from lack of equal opportunities as well as exploitation and abuse, men, in the long run, will profit the most from being *forced* to relate to liberated women. Men, freed of the pressures of the double standard and aggressive, ulcerous behavior, will

THE WOMEN'S LIBERATION MOVEMENT HAS A LOT TO SAY TO ALL OF US

Here is what we have to say:

be able to share responsibilities and bring harmony to the most disquieting, sexist aspects of our society.

Many people have come to associate the women's liberation movement only with specific issues, such as abortion on demand, day care, sharing household responsibilities, and equal opportunity in job employment. But liberation is much more than this. Liberation means that you are attempting to discover yourself in a realistic, rather than romanticized or culturally stereotyped, manner and then are *acting* on your discoveries. Explaining

The authentic meaning of the women's movement is related to equal opportunities for decision making, career choices, leisure time, and equal pay for equal work.

these new feelings and actions may be one of the most important bridges that men and women must build.

It is fashionable now for some women to say that they don't want to be liberated and for men to say that they want the old-fashioned, unliberated women to care for and endear in the manner of their worst impulses. It's too late to stop the most revolutionary movement of our times, and the men and women who struggle against this movement will suffer the terrible fate of boredom.

ON GIVING UP ONE'S CAREER TO SUPPORT YOUR MATE'S GETTING ONE

DON'T DO IT

Many people (mostly women) work their fingers to the bone (as secretaries, of course) to enable their husbands to complete their under- or post-graduate studies only to be abandoned and "exchanged" for a woman with a comparable degree.

THE BOREDOM OF UNLIBERATED WOMEN AND MEN

It is boring to relate to an unliberated woman.

Can you imagine after five years of marriage she still responds to your question, "What should we do tonight?" with "Anything you want to is fine with me, dear."

The unliberated man, of course, may pretend he enjoys this response, or it may be he who acquiesces. Regardless of who plays what role, though, it is exhausting to be with someone who constantly relies on you.

FOR THOSE OF YOU WHO SUFFER FROM SEXISM IN HIGH SCHOOL

The way to power is *organization*. One outspoken person is usually much more effective with a *group* behind her/him.

Young women can no longer afford to be routed into classes that exclude them from vocational skills, such as industrial arts. This is why: One-

third of the nation's breadwinners are women. *Most* female-headed families are well below the poverty line.

Therefore, if you want to prevent yourself from being considered "basically passive" by apathetic school authorities, your best bet is to start organizing consciousness-raising groups (among male students too) and to push for women's real needs and views to be expressed in your high school paper.

At this time you have several advantages: Women's liberation is beginning to gain acceptance even among Establishment types. There are many women, old and young, on the faculty who strongly sympathize with you, and some liberal male faculty members who might help.

Get with it.

Essential Book: *The New Our Bodies, Ourselves,* by the Boston Women's Collective (Simon & Schuster).

Margaret Sanger is one of my heroes.

September 14, 1979 was the 100th anniversary of her birth.

In the process of her pioneering work for legalization of birth control, she was constantly harassed by federal authorities. She took part in hundreds of street rallies and went to jail nine times. Margaret Sanger was the founder of Planned Parenthood. Her battle cry was:

"We must put our convictions into action."

MARGARET SANGER

Rebel in the Midst of Victorian Moralism

By TOBY A. CLINCH

September 14, 1979 was the 100th Anniversary of the birth of Margaret Higgins Sanger. Who was Margaret Sanger? The question was recently asked of 23 people attending a local community art center exhibition. Two individuals knew her as the founder of Planned Parenthood. The other 21 either made wild guesses, or had no idea.

Amazingly, in spite of the tremendous influence this woman has had on the life of almost every individual living today, Margaret Sanger is relatively unknown to many. Perhaps because information on, and practice of, birth control is so accepted and established, it is difficult to imagine that at one time, one individual spent 50 years fighting to secure this basic human right for every woman, and lived to see the battle won.

In the process of the campaign she waged, Mrs. Sanger was constantly harassed by Federal authorities, police raids, numerous indictments and lawsuits; she led and took part in hundreds of street rallies and went to jail nine times. No doubt this sounds as if it comes from the pages of history documenting the demonstrations of the 1960s. Actually, Mrs. Sanger's "notoriety" began in March 1914 with her publication of the first issues of *Woman Rebel* in which she announced (among other then-radical ideas) that the newspaper advocated the prevention of conception and "would impart such knowledge in the columns of this newspaper." Although contraceptive practices were not detailed, what she had written was apparently enough for the Post Office Department to declare the publication to be in violation of Section 211 of the Criminal Code of

the United States—a group of obscenity statutes drafted and hastily pushed through Congress in 1873 at the insistence of Anthony Comstock, founder and lifelong Secretary of the New York Society for the Suppression of Vice.

The Comstock Law, as it was to be popularly known, prohibited the mailing, transporting or importing of "obscene, lewd, or lascivious" materials, including information and devices concerned with "preventing conception." Congress unfortunately offered no guidelines or definitions to determine what was to be considered obscene; this judgment was left to the discretion of individual postal authorities, including the Post Master General's Special Agent, Anthony Comstock. Soon, twenty-two states had instituted their own Comstock-type statutes; the most stringent were those in Massachusetts and Connecticut.

Later issues of *Woman Rebel* (May, July, August, September and October) also were declared unmailable. The June issue was the first to use the phrase "birth control," a term Margaret Sanger and a few friends had devised. Ironically, this was the only edition the Post Office did not censor!

In August 1914 Margaret Sanger was indicted on nine counts for violating the Comstock Law. Mrs. Sanger failed to appear for her trial. With the flair for the dramatic that was to characterize her career, she fled the country, leaving behind her architect husband, William Sanger, and their three children.

Woman Rebel never gave contraceptive information. However, her secretly-printed pamphlet, "Family Limitation," did describe contraceptive techniques which included the use of douches, condoms, suppositories and cervical caps. She had planned to break and challenge the law banning the dissemination of contraceptive information and articles by distributing this pamphlet, but her court indictment was not based on the provisions of the Comstock Law that she had planned to challenge. Deeming it not advantageous to her cause, Mrs. Sanger left for Montreal and there, un-

der the assumed name of Bertha Watson, sailed for England. After three days at sea, using a pre-arranged code, she cabled word to release the 100,000 copies of "Family Limitation" which were strategically hidden in key cities around the U.S. They were distributed primarily through locals of the Industrial Workers of the World.

In England, Mrs. Sanger met, among others, H. G. Wells, the Drysdales (leaders of the Malthusian League), and the renowned sexual psychologist Havelock Ellis. Under the tutelage and guidance of Ellis and the Drysdales, Margaret Sanger learned to focus her ideas and energies, develop an ideological structure, philosophy and justification for the cause she was to pursue for the rest of her active life.

Two months after her arrival in England, Mrs. Sanger went to Holland to see the government-supported birth control clinic in operation. There she learned of the superior diaphragm developed by Dr. Wilhelm Mensinga in the 1880s and, most significantly, she learned that each woman wanting birth control must be medically examined and specially fitted with the appropriate type and size of diaphragm. In "Family Limitation" she advocated that women learn from pamphlets or teach each other. This cost her, at that time, the support and respect of the medical profession.

By then, Margaret Sanger had decided to spend the rest of her life promoting family planning. Why she came to this decision is really not known. What was it that motivated Margaret Sanger to champion the cause of birth control with such fervor and such exclusivity that it was to take precedence over everything—even her marriage and her children?

It could have been her poor beginnings on the banks of the Chemung River in Corning, New York, where she was the sixth-born child of a frail, submissive mother who died at the age of 48 after giving birth to 11 children. Her father, described by Mrs. Sanger as a "philosopher, a rebel and an artist," lived to the disparate age of 80.

Irish-born Michael Higgins, carver of

graveyard tombstones, a free-thinking, iconoclastic man who lived his socialist beliefs, was himself the champion of many then-radical causes. Throughout her childhood, Higgins fought and argued for socialism, women's suffrage, the single tax, free libraries, free education, free books in public schools, and freedom of the mind from dogma. In fact, his open resistance and dispute of the dogma of the Catholic Church in their predominantly Roman Catholic community caused his family extreme social and economic hardship. Poor as they were, though, Higgins provided his family with significant books—books Higgins believed would stimulate the imagination and promote thought. His credo, espoused to each of his children as they left home, was to leave the world better than they had found it.

Margaret Sanger may have gained other insights growing up in Corning. She could not help but notice and reflect on the disparity of the lives of the well-to-do people who lived up on the hill; they all had less children than the poorer families down near the river.

If not from her insights in Corning, Margaret Sanger's dedication could have come as a result of the suffering and death she witnessed when she worked as a nurse in the teeming tenements on New York's Lower East Side, where desperate women who didn't have the $5 to go to an abortionist punctured themselves with, among other things, knitting needles, to keep from having another baby. It was estimated at that time that 25,000 women died from abortions each year.

Undoubtedly, Margaret Sanger witnessed many deaths in the course of her work on the Lower East Side, but the one that seems to have had the most traumatic effect on her, the one incident that immediately preceded her resolve to discontinue her nursing profession and search for the truth about contraception, concerned Sadie Sachs. Mrs. Sachs was a woman whose life Mrs. Sanger and a doctor had worked laboriously to save after a self-induced abortion in the spring of

1912. Afterward, Mrs. Sachs pleaded with the doctor to tell her the "secret" of how to prevent another pregnancy. The only advice the doctor gave was a suggestion to have her husband, Jake, sleep on the roof. Margaret Sanger couldn't help Mrs. Sachs, any more than she was able to help the countless other women who had pleaded for the same information, because she didn't know the "secret" either. Three months later, in the fall of 1912, Sadie Sachs died from another attempted abortion. Margaret Sanger was the nurse in attendance. Afterward, Mrs. Sanger began her pursuit of the "secret."

For almost a year after the death of Sadie Sachs, Margaret Sanger visited dozens of libraries, including the Academy of Medicine and the Library of Congress to "ascertain something about the subject which was so mysterious and so unaccountably forbidden." She found, she claimed, "no information more reliable than that exchanged by back-fence gossips in any small town." At the suggestions of Bill Haywood, leader of the International Workers of the World and one of the coterie of well-known radicals, artists and intellectuals befriended by the Sangers soon after their move to New York City, Margaret decided to go to France, where family planning had been in practice since the Revolution, to learn about contraception. Going to Paris seemed to suit Bill Sanger, too. He had been talking about giving up building suburban houses in order to paint. To finance the trip, they sold their house in Hastings, where they had lived before moving to New York City, gave away some furniture, put the rest in storage, and sailed for Europe on a small, crowded, cabin boat.

Actually, there was a great deal of information on contraception available in America at that time. Casual research would have revealed the oldest recorded contraceptive information translated from ancient Egyptian documents dating back to 1850 B.C. More lucid and detailed accounts of contraceptive methods also appeared in the 2nd Century, A.D. in the writings of the Greek gynecologist Soranus of Ephesus. Robert

Dale Owens, a social reformer who was later to become a U.S. Congressman, offered in his 1830 *Moral Physiology* fairly crude but effective prescriptions to prevent pregnancy. The next truly comprehensive publication on contraceptive techniques, *The Fruits of Philosophy: or the Private Companion of Young Married People* by Dr. Charles Knowlton, a respected Boston physician, appeared in 1832, 47 years before Margaret Sanger was born!

In addition, the road to birth control was well paved by: Moses Harmon and his daughter Lillian, who edited and published the midwestern journal of sex radicalism, *Lucifer, the Light Bearer* from 1883–1907; Ezra and Angela Heywood who, in 1873, began publishing *The Word*, a journal dedicated to the abolition of woman's slavery; Dr. Edward Bliss Foote, and later his son, Dr. Edward Bond "Ned" Foote, who wrote and published, in 1858, the best seller *Medical Common Sense* which contained two essays on pregnancy preventions and explanations of various contraceptives (two for men and two for women). One pamphlet, "Words in Pearl," published in 1873, described contraceptive techniques and devices, and told how to obtain them.

In 1898, the *Index Catalogue of the Library of the Surgeon-General's Office* contained two pages listing the articles and books available on pregnancy prevention. And, interestingly, in 1912, the same year Margaret Sanger researched information on pregnancy prevention, Dr. Abraham Jacobi, founder of the *American Journal of Obstetrics and Diseases of Children*, and the man who made pediatrics a specialty in this country, openly espoused family planning in his presidential address to the American Medical Association.

Was Margaret Sanger denied access to all this material? Or did she choose to suppress or ignore it? The answer can only be left to conjecture. Some who have known Margaret Sanger, and some who have written about her, contend that her dedication to the birth control movement was a result of her vanity, her need to be the central figure, a rebel demanding attention to her exploits and to be recognized as the sole leader of the birth control movement.

In January 1914, Margaret Sanger did, indeed, return to the U.S. and dramatically made preparations to introduce her collection of formulas, techniques and devices she had learned about from Parisian doctors, midwives, druggists and women. It was this information that was contained in her pamphlet "Family Limitation," which before long had been translated into 13 languages, reaching a circulation of over 10 million. While berated by some of her techniques, it must be recognized that her actions did have impact; they made many aware that compared to France, America still lived in the Dark Ages, and it made many women cognizant of the birth control movement as well as the existence of birth control methods.

Though dramatic and unorthodox techniques were to characterize Mrs. Sanger's career, she was hardly the typical firebrandishing, foot-stomping, harassing, blustering female reformer. Most people who met her were rather surprised by her conservative dress, her soft-spoken voice and her personal charm. New York University Professor, and social scientist, Henry Pratt Fairchild, in the *Nation*, described her as "a rather slight woman, very beautiful, with wide-apart gray eyes and a crown of auburn hair, combining a radiant feminine appeal with an impression of serenity, calm, and graciousness of voice and manner . . . [*but with*] tremendous fighting spirit . . . self-generating energy, and . . . relentless drive . . ." It was her charisma and her intelligence that made a great many converts to the birth control movement.

Even her husband, Bill Sanger, who had returned to America just before Mrs. Sanger fled to England, was converted to the cause. While Mrs. Sanger was in England, Anthony Comstock, posing as an impoverished father seeking means of preventing pregnancy, visited Bill Sanger who gave him a copy of "Family Limitation." Sanger was arrested and convicted on obscenity charges. Instead of paying the fine, however, he chose to go to jail for 30 days. This was the test case Margaret Sanger had wanted; her exile was over. Risking a prison sentence on her own criminal charges, she returned home.

The climate for Mrs. Sanger's trial was right. Bill Sanger had become a hero and a martyr to the cause, and the magazine headline that greeted Mrs. Sanger when she arrived in New York harbor read, "What Shall We Do About Birth Control?" And, in New York City, the first American birth control organization, the National Birth Control League, had formed under the direction of Mary Ware Dennett. But less than four weeks after her arrival, before her case was reopened, tragedy struck—a personal tragedy from which Margaret Sanger never quite recovered—the death of her youngest child and only daughter, Peggy, from pneumonia. Shattered and suffering a nervous breakdown, Mrs. Sanger nevertheless was determined to face the indictments against her, even though they dealt not with contraception, but with articles in *Woman Rebel* concerning assassination, feminine hygiene and marriage. Her lawyers all advised compromise; if she pleaded guilty, she would get off with a suspended sentence, or if she wrote a letter saying she would not break the law again, she would not even have to go to court. Margaret Sanger would not compromise.

Disgusted with her lawyers, Mrs. Sanger decided to appear in court without counsel. Meanwhile, public opinion had begun to swing toward her. The judge and district attorney were besieged by petitions and letters. President Woodrow Wilson had received scores of letters, some from England's most prominent people, including H. G. Wells, who pleaded in behalf of free speech. With all this public concern, the government suddenly seemed reluctant to prosecute, and without any explanation, and after several postponements, dismissed the case.

Margaret Sanger had won a moral victory, but the law had not been tested. Her next move was to dramatize and focus attention on the obsolete laws. To do this, she set out on a speaking tour, criss-crossing the country. Her tour served several purposes—it attracted a devoted group of followers, inspired opposition, and caused possibly millions of people to talk about her.

Returning to New York, Mrs. Sanger put another of her plans into action. This she did with her sister, Mrs. Ethel Byrne, also a registered nurse, and another woman, Fania Mindell. On October 16, 1916, to implement all she had learned in Holland she opened America's first birth control clinic at 46 Amboy Street in the poor, heavily populated Brownsville section of Brooklyn. After distributing flyers (in Italian, Yiddish and English), advertising the services offered, the clinic opened for business. At 7 a.m., the line of women stretched around the block; they saw 140 women that first day. Newspapers carried the story, and dozens of women came from as far away as Pennsylvania, Massachusetts and Connecticut.

Ten days after they opened their doors, the three clinic operators were arrested. Released on bail, the women reopened the clinic. Again they were arrested, and this time the clinic closed for good. The arrests were made under Section 1142 of the New York State Penal Code, which made it a misdemeanor for anyone to "sell, lend or give away" contraceptive devices. Section 1145 of the code made exception to Section 1142 in the cases of physicians, who *were* permitted to advise and prescribe articles "for the care and prevention of disease." Most physicians interpreted this to apply only to venereal disease. However, there was no physician in attendance at the clinic.

Margaret Sanger and her sister each were sentenced to 30 days in jail for "maintaining a public nuisance." Mrs. Sanger chose to spend that time teaching the women she met about contraception, and issuing statements to the press about the deplorable prison conditions. Mrs. Byrne, on the other hand, went on a hunger strike and accounts of her "forced feeding" through a tube inserted in her esophagus made front-page headlines, alongside news of the war in Europe. The publicity enhanced Mrs. Sanger's cause tremendously and paved the way for the appeal of her conviction in the N.Y. Supreme Court. Although her conviction was upheld, Judge J. Crane did broaden the interpretation of Section 1145, allowing physicians to legally prescribe contraceptive devices and give advice to married people in N.Y. state for health reasons, not only to prevent venereal disease.

Public education, Mrs. Sanger reasoned, was the next logical step in furthering the birth control cause. Along with speaking engagements, she launched, with the help of Frederick A. Blossom, a leader in the Ohio Birth Control League, the *Birth Control Review* to keep the movement apprised of various birth control activities. Much of her time was spent in fund-raising activities, and promoting the *Birth Control Review,* which she personally hawked on N.Y. street corners.

The year 1920 was a noteworthy one for Margaret Sanger. Her marriage to Bill Sanger ended in divorce; they had been separated for seven years. And the first of two books she had been working on, *Women and the New Race*, was published, selling over 200,000 copies. Her other book, *The Pivot of Civilization*, appeared two years later. Both books, which contained every conceivable rationale for birth control, were read all over the world and lent an air of respectability to the movement. They also served to establish Margaret Sanger as the unofficial leader of the birth control movement.

Margaret Sanger died on September 6, 1966, eight days before her 87th birthday. She was one of the few crusaders in the world who lived long enough to see her dreams become a reality. Ironically, after over 60 years of efforts, the Comstock Law, the statutes Margaret Sanger worked so tirelessly to nullify, are still Federal Law, though all of the birth control and most of the other restrictions they imposed have been modified by judicial interpretation. It is as the brilliant civil rights attorney, Morris Ernst, has said, "In the United States

we almost never repeal outmoded legislation in the field of morals. We either allow it to fall into disuse by ignoring it . . . or we bring persuasive cases to the courts and get the obsolete laws modified by judicial interpretation." And such is the situation concerning the Comstock Law in 1979, 100 years after the birth of Margaret Sanger.

Toby A. Clinch is a freelance writer currently residing in Australia. She is the author of many articles on sexuality including "The Great Comic Book Controversy."

MARGARET SANGER   1979

        dear Margaret
did you
        know
        Albert Einstein
was also born a hundred years ago?
        do you think that if
you two
got together
        it would have made a
difference to the world?

        You were a courageous champion
for Planned Parenthood
        He was the brilliant scientist
and humanist

We understand more for
        the lives of you two
        but we are not much further along

Talk it over with Albert, Margaret

        I hope you are not as disappointed
as I sometimes am. You did the best you could.
        We should have paid more attention
but the same people who attacked both of you are still at it.

IF YOU EVER

Become A Parent

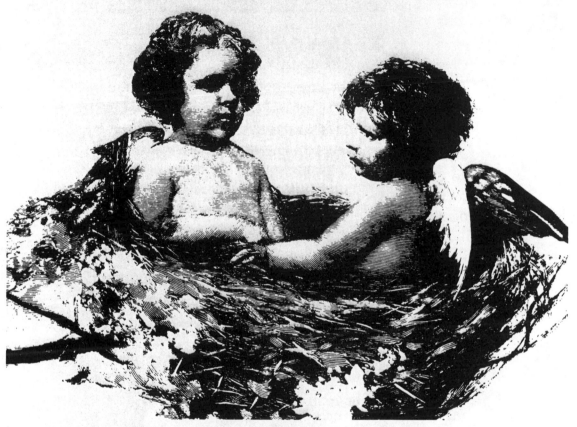

Do It Right Your Time Around

Despite rumors, "scientific" research and popular "Y we R like we R" books, some psychologists like myself readily admit that we don't really know why people turn out the way they do. Too many of us have seen rotten, self-destructive kids come from what seem to us to be reasonably, if not perfectly, mature families. (Of course, the more fancy among us can always come up with some kind of unconscious or latent hostility to explain everything.) And we have seen really terrific kids emerge from rotten, self-destructive families. The plain fact is that some kids are more adequate than the families that nurture them.

Life is complex. We don't really know how much influence parents have in contrast with brothers and sisters; nor whether stable mothers working outside the home are more effective than nervous mothers at home all the time; nor how much input comes from TV, peers, living in a materialistic society, and what have you. There are a few things we seem to know, however. Children exposed to extremes, such as rejection or smother love, don't turn out very well. Children brought up in a poverty-stricken, crime-ridden neighborhood get into more trouble with the law and tend not to earn as much money when they grow up as do children brought up in the affluent suburbs.

Self-confidence and feelings of adequacy are transmitted by adults who are confident and comfortable with their impulses. But too often, our society and culture operate in opposition to the impulse life of the child. Many mothers seem to have developed child-rearing practices based on notions inspired by popular women's magazines. Fifteen years ago we were supposed to be strict with children; ten years ago we were supposed to be permissive. Today, we don't love them enough, but are allowed to beat them occasionally. Ten years ago a schedule was all the rage; three years later we were supposed to feed permissively. Recently, it was discovered that fathers are important.

I have seen homes where the parents were strict, homes where the parents were permissive, and other homes where both parents were neurotic. In all these cases the children have been perfectly normal. But children do grow up confused, unhappy, and neurotic when the mother is insecure about her role as a mother, or when there is conflict between the mother and father about the child. Parents have become confused by an overabundance of advice from magazines, from their own mothers and fathers, and from neighbors. As a result, many parents cannot respond in a spontaneous way to their own children.

One of the most dynamic results of spontaneity is the courage to accept the impulse life of the child. Let me illustrate some of the ways we might respond to children's impulses.

A child has a nightmare. S/he wakes up in terrible fear and screams for mother. The mother might say, "Oh, there's nothing to be afraid of." But the child is frightened. What we need to say to the child is, "Yes, it is very frightening to have a nightmare." Then we must reassure him/her that s/he is loved and not alone.

Another example: Jimmy is six, his brother Johnny is four, and Jimmy doesn't like his brother. Mother says, "But you're supposed to like your brother, he *is* your brother," as though this has any meaning to the child. This mother could be saying "You don't have to like your brother, but I still don't want you to hit him."

Sandra is seven and comes home from her first day in school and says, "I don't like my teacher, she is a nut." Too often, Mother replies, "Oh, you mustn't say that!" As a matter of fact, Sandra may be right.

121

Why are we unable to accept the free, spontaneous statements of children? They are often correct. Spontaneity is mental health in action. Acceptance provides the child with a sense of security. Children who are secure will learn in school with a good teacher or a poor one. Characteristic of a secure child is his inner striving to become a more complete person. Characteristic of the maladjusted child is his struggle against his mother, his father, and other authority figures.

Of course, not only should parents be able to talk freely with each other, but they must also be able to respond to their children's questions as they are asked and not work on the assumption that the less a child knows the better off s/he is. The opposite is true.

It is also not possible to tell a child too much. Children simply ignore or are bored by knowledge they cannot understand—they'll turn you off. Contrary to what some people think, information doesn't stimulate socially inappropriate behavior. Ignorance does.

Besides, what neighbor has ever worried that *his/her* kid will tell *your* kid the cock-and-bull story about the cabbage leaf or Mr. Stork? It's time that the kids whose parents have given the correct facts become the sex educators in their own neighborhoods.

SPECIAL ALERT

Don't have children mainly to satisfy your parents' "grandparent" complex or to bolster a deflated ego (no child can blow it up for you).

Have children for the sheer joy of it, knowing full well that it can also be a drag. And once they are grown, know that you will never have the control over them you think you should have or deserve to have.

Consider Tommy, a nine-year-old, who is caught drawing a "dirty" picture. His mother gets very excited. She snatches the picture from the boy's hands. (In this country, you need evidence.) Apart from disturbing Tommy, she has revealed to her son that she has a sex problem. She calls in her husband, who also gets very excited, indicating that he, too, is threatened by the question of sex.

Consider the parent who is terribly orderly and preoccupied with cleanliness. Anyone preoccupied with cleanliness worries about dirt most of the time. Why project your concern with dirt upon children? If children feel that their thoughts are dirty, their ideas dirty, and their behavior dirty, they end up feeling guilty and insecure.

Having said all that, we must say that most parents mean well and want to bring up their children so they can be happy, creative, self-supporting members of society.

Because most of you reading this will marry (despite your best intentions) and will bring into this world at least one, probably two children (despite the fact that you may be happier without children), we would like to offer some advice about doing it right your time around (which, as you know, will be difficult to do even if you want to).

1 First, talk to your spouse about advantages and disadvantages of having children and decide about the timing. Plan and agree about sharing responsibilities in advance. (While it's not always a disaster to have an unplanned child, it often is.)

2 Both you and your spouse should read Dr. Spock—and Lee Salk's parenting book—if you want to get into it heavy, or my parenting book if you want to get into it light.

3 Decide that you don't have to do everything right to be a good parent, and be willing to admit to your children that you are not always right even if you think you are not often wrong.

4 Realize that open, genuine affection for each is probably the most important gift you can offer your children.

5 Appreciate that bringing up a creative child has little to do with prescribed or predetermined standards of performance. Creativity usually means that parents will have to allow for some lapses in discipline.

6 One good way to test your readiness for parenthood is to consider your attitudes toward sex.

Here are the main things
we think you should know
(in a nutshell, of course)
about educating your children about sex.

Masturbation: Playing with one's genitals is a common and normal activity for children and should not be a source for scolding, punishment or milder forms of disapproval, such as substituting a toy. The child needs to explore her/his body and should not be discouraged from doing so. As the child gets older (say three or four) s/he can be taught to masturbate only in private.

Nudity: Nudity in the bath and bedroom is a healthy introduction to sexual differences and sexuality. The child will let his parents know when his/her modesty dictates privacy by closing the door, or asking to bathe alone, etc. Parental privacy needs to be protected too, sometimes.

Proper Terminology: Giving correct names for parts of the body is important. It's just as easy to teach a little boy "penis" as it is "ding-a-ling," or "bowel movement" or "b.m." rather than "poo-poo" or some other term. Similarly, a child should know the correct words for sexual intercourse and sexual behavior.

Obscenity: If a child repeats a word that s/he heard in the street or from adults, use the word, and explain what it means. This approach has several advantages. First, your child will know s/he can't use it as a weapon against you. Second, the child will realize that such questions won't make you uptight. Third, by explaining it with proper terminology you are treating the subject of sex with respect, instead of relegating it to the street.

Touching: Children often grow up with the feeling that touching and expressing affection are inappropriate. This attitude develops primarily because they rarely see adults *touch*. Consequently, they grow up not knowing how to express themselves physically. As teenagers, they will believe that touching another person is only a prelude to sexual intercourse. Parents should not cut off physical affection from their children after infancy, because a child still needs this physical reassurance of his/her parent's love.

TOWARD A SUCCESSFUL MARRIAGE

Ninety-three percent of us are married or will marry at some time in our lives. There are indications that the current one-in-two divorce rate may be leveling off. Even so, four out of every five divorced adults eventually remarry. Despite statistics, theories, and pressures from within and without, millions of us, trusting our hearts and our hopes, simply refuse to let marriage die. The problem today is neither how to resurrect a fallen institution nor how to swing the nonconformist seven percent into line, but how to think about marriage, how to prepare for it, and behave within it so as to enhance of our lives.

The clear trend today is in the direction of egalitarian marriages in which both partners tend to find greater stability, more excitement, and a heightened sense of worth in themselves and in each other.

To the family of tomorrow, husband and wife will bring comparable education. Both will work outside the home for the greater portion of their adult lives. Of those who consciously decide to have children, a majority will stop at two. Parenthood will be a shared experience with both partners taking major responsibility for child care.

People will marry because they love and care for each other. They will have children because they want to. They will not allow the desire for money or prestige to push them into ill-considered alliances. They will not marry to legitimize unplanned pregnancies. They will not subordinate their own feelings and preferences in a futile quest for parental approval. Without all that excess baggage, without the guilt, fear, and uncertainty that return to haunt so many relationships today, tomorrow's parents will be far better able to meet and enjoy the challenge of marriage, child-rearing, and work.

Why do so many of today's families break apart? Most of the time it has very little to do with sexual maladjustments or with the presumed emergent aggressiveness on the part of women. It is much the same reason that old relationships disintegrate. It is boredom and inequality.

People who marry for the wrong reasons, whose expectations are unrealistic and immature, will sooner or later grow terribly bored with each other. What—when two people live in the same house, sleep in the same bed, and eat at the same table every day—could possibly be worse? An occasional

*This section is for not-yet marrieds and not-optimally successful marrieds and anyone else who would like my opinion about marriage.

episode of impotence? A redistribution of a few household chores? These and similar disruptions do not threaten the bond between two people who love each other. But boredom not only threatens a relationship, it can destroy it.

There are those who cry for a return to traditional values, and others who claim that successful pursuit of the ultimate, multiple, simultaneous orgasm will solve everything. But such "remedies" for marital distress are bankrupt and unworkable. They fail to address the fundamental questions: Do we love and care about each other? Do we *interest* each other?

> *Happiness is found along the way not at the end of the road.*

Some of the harshest critics of the women's liberation movement are forever warning us about the dangers of a generation of "aggressive women." It seems to me a far more serious danger awaits those who accept such scare talk and creep back inside their houses. Of course women *are* becoming more assertive. But assertiveness is nothing more than the pursuit of self-respect. It does not suggest a particular style of clothing or tone of voice or political orientation. Think about it. Have you ever done something that made you feel good about yourself and then worried that in the process you lost respect in the eyes of other people? True assertive behavior increases self-esteem; the more you have cause to respect yourself, the more other people have cause to agree.

Assertive women (and men) can protect their interests without resorting to aggressive or "pushy" behavior. In caricature, the aggressive woman dressed in heavy overalls punches her boss in the face, and demands a raise. In truth, the assertive woman dressed attractively in her own style, confronts her boss with a statement of fact and purpose: "I am here to ask for a raise for the following reasons." Women, whose legitimate rights are not realized, have every reason to become aggressive.

To illustrate from my own marriage, I hate doing any kind of housework, but I do it now because I have an assertive wife. I didn't want her to become aggressive. (Incidentally, I was quite surprised to get her message that she dislikes housework every bit as much as I do.)

What exactly does it mean to say that men have become liberated? Again, it has nothing to do with dress, manner, or politics. It is that state of mind in which a man is not threatened by his partner's growing self-respect or legitimate ambition. It is mature and accommodating; in large part it is what makes healthy relationships work.

Before turning specifically to the qualities that characterize dynamic and exciting marriages—relationships between liberated and assertive partners—I offer, first, a few ground rules, not in any particular order.

1. The *quality* of marriage need not in any major way be affected by a couple's decision about children. The important thing is for two people to develop their relationship with each other first, before children are born or even contemplated, and to reassess and reaffirm that relationship often through the years whatever the decision about children has been. Thus, my list will make no references to children.

2. There is no end to new beginnings. Even the most tiresome marriage can be salvaged. To be sure, the passage of time in itself does very little except to make us older. But it's amazing how time *and* effort *and* genuine mutual desire for change can bring new happiness and interest into a relationship.

3. One "sure" test of marital happiness is your energy level. Good marriages are energizing. There is time for everything—or almost everything. Happily married people do not scurry about all day long in a hyperactive frenzy, but they do have the will and energy to be creative and productive. Bad marriages and immature relationships are exhausting for both partners.

4. For all the screeching about so-called liberated women, the fact is that liberation in its truest sense becomes and enhances those who embrace it. What best distinguishes liberated adults of both sexes from their unliberated neighbors is their freedom to behave, and to behave *well*, to be interesting and interested, to be alternately warm and businesslike, dependent and daring, needed and in need. Liberated men and women have dignity. They do not feel inferior to others; they will not let themselves be made to feel inferior. At the same time, they are delighted to praise the real achievements of other people.

Those who do not assert their rights will inevitably find their husbands and wives spending less and less time with them. Nobody wants to be bored. To avoid it we drag ourselves bowling on Monday, play cards on Tuesday, watch movies all night on Wednesday, hit the bars on Friday. . . .

5. Marriage without passion may be dull, but without friendship it is devastating.

6. Conspicuous by their absence from this list are offerings to such familiar goddesses as fidelity, exclusivity, total honesty, owning, belonging, total sharing, and "meant for each other."

7. I believe in love but not when it becomes a burden, in priority not exclusivity, in sharing not soul purges, in deeds not promises. There has to be space within the context of commitment. Without it, self-indulgence and exploitation will take root and grow.

Fair enough, you say, but what do all these words look like in real life?

THE BIG 10
(in order of importance)

1. Love—caring, intimacy, loyalty, and trust during good times and bad, holding strong in the face of illness or stress. It includes such simple things as remembering birthdays and anniversaries and ordinary courtesies, offering help without being asked, saying "I love you."

2. Learning how and when to laugh—having a sense of humor and keeping it tuned. You had one when you were little. Where did it go? If living were a series of traumatic episodes, laughter wouldn't be practical. But there are very few real traumas in life. It isn't necessary to be downcast so much of the time. Learn to laugh. Practice.

3. Making interesting conversation—being sensitive to the interests of your partner, sparing him the office gossip, sparing her the traffic situation on Interstate 80. The key here is the willingness to communicate. Don't be afraid of hurting your partner's feelings or of revealing your own. Express your own point of view. If your partner doesn't share it, nothing is lost. If he explains why, so much the better.

4. Together, a passionate sense of mission or purpose about something(s)—an involvement with other people's lives as a means of enhancing your own. It can be anything—a "cause," your religion, the environment, politics.

5. Friends together and separately—sharing time and talk with people you both enjoy, being sensitive to the negative chemistry between your partner and some of your dearest friends. Learn to cherish some space, privacy, interests, hobbies, and even an occasional vacation of your own.

6. A promise— you will not compromise the person you want to be, you are not negotiable. Do what it pleases you to do (this category may be nowhere near as large as you might at first think). If you want to have children and stay home with them while they're small, if you'd rather work away from home, or if you want to balance work and family, *do it*, and with no apologies. If someone expresses disapproval, says you're wasting your time, it's not your problem unless you agree. In this respect it might not be a bad idea to declare a moratorium on analyzing. If you're reasonably happy with whatever it is you do, why look for reasons to reconsider?

7. Tolerance—for occasional craziness, irritableness, tiredness, clumsiness, memory lapses, human error, disagreement, argument, and very contrary points of view.

8. Willingness to accept each other's style—active in some respects, passive in others. Don't be bound by fixed or predetermined notions that X is always a female prerogative or Y always a male imperative. A man can change diapers, tend sick children, respond with pleasure to a woman's sexual initiatives. A woman can change a tire, bring home the biggest paycheck, get the first (or only) Ph.D. in the house.

9. Sexual fulfillment—not measured in terms of orgasmic frequency or quality, but as an abiding expression of shared intimacy. It is possible for people who hate each other to have good mechanical sex. And there are loving, devoted couples whose coital positionings leave much to be desired. While the sex machines may never learn to like each other, the caring partners can learn to overcome their sexual difficulties—by relaxing and by forgoing intercourse for a while in favor of simple touching, truthful talk about what gives pleasure, a shower for two, listening to music.

Sex is the most grossly overstated "privilege" of marriage. Even today we still hear righteous warnings that sex before marriage leaves nothing to look forward to. To those who perceive sex as the main benefit of marriage I'd advise them not to marry. It's not worth it.

10. Sharing household tasks—I clean, you cook; I fold, you iron; I mow, you rake. Next week reverse it, or not, as it suits you both.

So, there it is—unadorned. Has anything major been left out? Is the order right? Let me know what you think.

I remember one irate man who, on hearing this list, could not believe that sexual fulfillment placed so near the bottom. I replied that of the 5,325 important aspects of marriage, sex was still in the top 10. (Not bad!)

Of course very few marriages are in an optimal state all or even most of the time. Ebbs and flows, ups and downs, are part of the human condition. But the partners in good marriages find happiness in striving toward it. This isn't Pollyanna-style gaiety, all sweetness and light with never a blessed break, but a sensible optimism, buoyant and energetic, for at least a part of every day. After all, most meaningful peak experiences are of brief duration—a certain look in someone's eyes, sunset, a baby's first cry. The rest of the time most of us are just too busy to be analyzing ourselves.

Marriage might best be seen as a journey in which two people together, and at times separately, discover all the other things in life they can offer each other. There is a growing sense that the past is past and that life is not a meaning but an opportunity for meaningful experiences. While traditions, rituals, observances, and flexible roles can give marriage structure and purpose, they can never substitute for loving, caring, kindness, loyalty, and having fun together.

Whom Not to Marry (if You Do Marry)

Everybody gives advice on *whom* to marry. Few listen. So we'll advise you on *whom not* to marry. Maybe you'll consider it.

Don't marry if one or more of the following conditions exist:

[1] If one of you relentlessly asks questions like, "Do you love me?" or "Do you really care about me?"

[2] If when you are together you spend most of your time disagreeing and quarreling (even if you miss each other when you are not together).

[3] If you don't really know each other as persons, even though you have spent a great deal of time together.

[4] If you are both still very young (roughly under 20). Most young marriages end in divorce or separation.

[5] You are marrying mainly to get away from your own home and family or to have someone "mother" you.

[6] If you find that your decision to get married has been largely influenced by your prospective father-in-law or mother-in-law. (Don't laugh! Not a few young people are led into matrimony by the warm acceptance, the flattery, the wealth, or even the cooking of a potential in-law.)

[7] If you keep having thoughts like, "Maybe things will be better after we're married," or your prospective mate insists on a particular behavior you don't like before marriage and promises "to change" after marriage. It rarely happens.

[8] If your fiancé has behavior traits that you can't stand (such as nonstop talking) and you avoid the issue for fear of giving offense.

[9] If your partner insists that you drop all your old friends and start afresh.

[10] If, after you've given it some thought, you discover you are marrying a sex object, not a person. A "showpiece" marriage becomes unbelievably boring after a while.

[11] Whatever you do, don't marry to "cover" an untimely pregnancy, especially if your main motive is to "do the right thing."

MENTAL ILLNESS

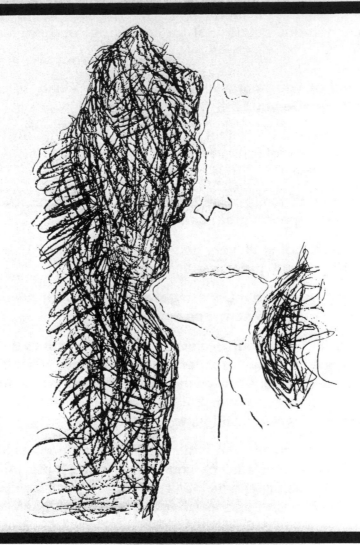

IF YOU THINK
YOU MIGHT
BE GOING CRAZY

For one thing, nobody is in perfect mental health. But the important thing is that there is a difference between an emotional problem and mental illness. You can hardly hope to get through life without suffering from some emotional hassles, just as you can't think that your body will never catch a virus.

When you are going through an emotional disorder, part of your constructive energies is knocked out, but you still manage to hang in there somehow.

People who are mentally ill are so disoriented that they are almost completely unable to care for themselves, or, if they do get by, they find it almost impossible to take care of anyone else for long.

Although most people don't talk about it, just about everyone you know has a relative who is or has been in a mental hospital. (Just as almost everyone has a relative who is alcoholic and/or who has committed suicide.)

Just because Uncle Joe is mentally ill doesn't mean you will become psychotic, even if you have some of his mannerisms. Sometimes members of your family may make remarks such as: "Now you're acting just like Uncle Joe." So what? Don't let such remarks mean anything.

IF YOU THINK SOMEBODY ELSE IS CRAZY

Some people who are called "mentally ill" are not. Sometimes people are committed to institutions just because they are going through a temporary period of confusion, or are an emotional burden on their families, or are threatening to relatives and neighbors because of "odd" or "out of character" behavior.

People with unpopular or disturbing ideas may be shut out by being branded "mentally ill."

Sometimes mentally retarded individuals are accused of being crazy. Only a very ignorant or a very insecure person would make such a judgment.

MOST IMPORTANT FACTS ABOUT MENTAL ILLNESS

- Mentally ill people can and do recover.
- The more a mentally ill person is mistreated or ignored, the less chance s/he has.
- The mentally ill person, whether s/he or others know it or not, is suffering from enormous mental anguish. The mentally ill person has an extraordinarily difficult time accepting intimacy with anyone. Many mentally ill people have abandoned hope—and this keeps them sick.

133

SUICIDE

Almost everyone at times has thoughts of suicide. Having such thoughts now and then does not mean you are suicidal or mentally ill.

Suicide may be "the decision to end all decisions," a response to overwhelming pain (sometimes physical, but usually mental), a result of overdosing on alcohol or drugs (frequently in combinations), or it may have been an accident.

Remember:

1. If life is so overwhelming that you are seriously thinking about murdering yourself, first do something constructive, such as summoning up all your strength to say a prayer (it can't hurt). Then call up a friend. If you can't do that, call up a hotline. If you can't do that, write a letter to a newspaper. Do something constructive. Think about this: If you are alive, that—all by itself—is good.
2. Overdoses of drugs and/or alcohol can weaken your inner strength to the point that you are at the mercy of your unconscious. Many people have gone berserk and destroyed themselves after downing speed, barbiturates, and alcohol.
3. Sometimes people will threaten to commit suicide as a desperate way of crying for help. What they want is attention, not death. But it may happen that while they are teetering on the bridge they lose their balance, or they turn on the gas and close the windows, but the expected relative doesn't show up at the usual time.

WHEN SOMEONE THREATENS SUICIDE

Obviously, anyone who makes an attempt at suicide needs immediate professional attention.

However, people who *talk* about suicide (even if casually or jokingly)—often have been going through some very unpleasant experiences. If no one takes them seriously and instead says things like, "That's silly" or "I'll join you" or other self-conscious remarks, these people become convinced that no one really cares enough to ask what's wrong. It is most helpful to take an active concern in the person by communicating: "Listen, you've been threatening to kill yourself lately and I'm very concerned—can we talk about it?" If the person is not responsive, you might call up your local suicide prevention center. Most cities have an emergency service (often it is listed as Contact). Read my book, *When Living Hurts.*

DEATH

Almost everybody seems to be into death these days. The whole idea bores me. Sure, we need to appreciate it as a part of life. But to study it, prepare for it, even praise the sick parts of other cultures that glory in it, seems deadly to me.

Dead should certainly not be considered a four-letter word. It's more like sad, a three-letter word.

We feel it powerfully when someone close to us dies. And the grief and the mourning are part of caring for ourselves and sharpen our own respect for life.

From a psychological standpoint, the most important fact to know about the death of a member of your immediate family is: Your first impulse is to feel guilty about it.

It's all right to have regrets that perhaps you didn't do enough for or weren't kind enough to someone. But don't let such a feeling hang you up for too long. Look at it this way: If you feel bad that your relationship with this person wasn't as good as you would like, the only thing that makes sense is to improve your relationships with those around you who are living.

Many people carry around a burden of *irrational* guilt after the death of a loved one. For example, the daughter who was away at college when her mother died becomes obsessed with the idea that maybe it would have turned out differently if only she had stayed home.

Don't freeze on that first impulse to feel guilty. People often die at unexpected and inopportune times. That's part of life. Again: Your obligation is to the living.

The part of death that horrifies me is the wanton, fierce murder of millions of people—a holocaust. That is worth studying. In the forgetting, we become accomplices.

Sure, there is a lot more to it, because a response to a death is so deeply personal. And that's the way I'd like to leave it.

135

"Oh what a Gem Lies buried here."

This is

the Grave

of

LAURA,

The wife of Harvey Baldwin

and daughter of

the Hon. James Geddes &

Lucy Geddes. She died

Oct. 18, 1825, aged

21 years.

In less than one revolving year, She was a Maid, a Bride, a Corpse,
Adorned with every grace, & possessing every personal
Charm & mental excellence,

"In her spring time She flew
to that land, where the wings of the Soul are unfurled,

And now, like a Star, beyond evenings cold dew,
Looks radiantly down on the tears of this
world."

This monument was erected to her memory
by her Husband, whom She loved.

Is Religion Dead?

"Here I am."

— Abraham

What's At The Bottom of Your Beliefs?

Is religion too phony, too incredible, or too heavy for you? If you don't have a religion you enjoy, or if you've rejected the religion of your parents, why not figure out your own religion? It's really good to believe in something. But that doesn't mean you shouldn't be cautious when it comes to religious ideas. After all, if your religion gives you nothing to think about, it doesn't offer much.

And if you don't think about the basis of your moral beliefs, you make way for the self-righteous hypocrites to set themselves up as the guardians of *your* (and everybody else's) morality. It's no accident that certain unscrupulous leaders make a big show of their religion. They'll tell you what to think and what to believe—if you let them.

Part of living in a democracy is having respect for the values of other people. To take an extra-sensitive example: Abortion. While we don't favor abortion as a method of birth control, we believe that *compelling* someone to give birth is evil. As it happens, most Americans agree with the Supreme Court's ruling that lawmakers may not interfere with a woman's right to have an abortion in the first twelve weeks of her pregnancy. Some people are flatly opposed to abortion. They have a right to express their feeling. But that does not give them the right to make abortion illegal.

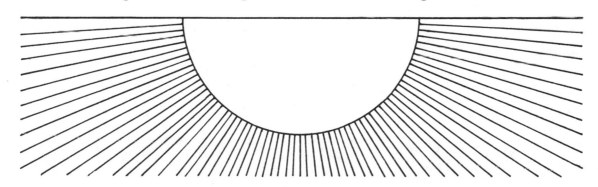

The real test of your religion is the effect it has in your personal life. Does it make you a better person?

Being a better person means:

1. You feel good about yourself, but still want to grow.
2. You can say: "I am." Being alive requires no justification.

This permits you to care for and love others.

A better person doesn't manipulate and exploit people, and balances selfish interests with the needs of others.

A better person strives for good relationships, intimacy (with one or more people), and to contribute as a citizen of the community and the world.

We will still be mean, selfish, and inconsiderate at times, but most often won't feel the need to hold a grudge, carry feuds to the extreme or antagonize people we don't get along with or don't know.

Test your own religion, or the basis for your moral beliefs, in the above terms. If it doesn't make sense, maybe you have not understood the message that no religion is motionless. New and different understandings take place through inspired/inspiring leaders and one's own inspirations, vibrations and revelations.

AN APOTHEOSIS TO MY LORD

If God is dead He must have Been
If He was, He is
If He is, He could not have Been

God		YOU
Is		ARE
Not Free		Free
To Tell	You	To
YOU	Must	Respond
What To		To
Do	Find	Him
	Your	Or
	Own	Her
	Way	

RANDOM THOUGHTS ON ROSH HASHANA* 5735

We all have some areas of vulnerability. Not everything in life can be understood or resolved.

I feel that just about everything really worthwhile in life involves some risk and some sacrifice of time, energy and patience.

I suspect that really meaningful experiences are of brief duration (albeit repeatable) and rarely occur on schedule.

Even tragic events offer us opportunities for review and renewal.

Some people are strange. If they don't understand something, they think it either doesn't exist or it isn't worthwhile.

If God wants to test you, what will you do?

*The Jewish New Year

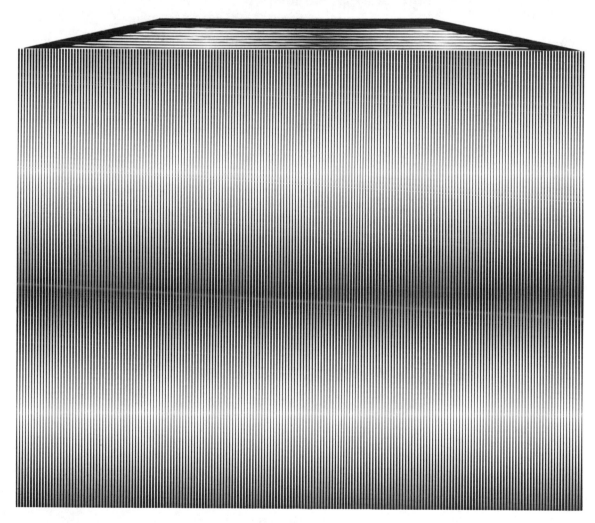

VARIETIES OF RELIGIOUS EXPERIENCE

I

Prayer for the dead

Whenever I think about dead people I care about
they get points up there

It's an irrational idea
but somehow I'm comforted
by the thoughts of my parents
scoring in the celestial heavens.

II

God won't stand for it

What's the point of finding God
If you can't find anyone else?

You can't use God to
validate who you are
(God won't stand for it)

III

Is Your Religion Organized?

Being religious isn't worth much
if God doesn't help you
become a friend
to at least one other person
and a member of a society
that cares about people.

140

IV

There Is a Way for Everyone

People who want to
mock God
    say there is only
    one road to Him

Lord knows, for Him
    a one-way sign is a
    dead end
    leading to nowhere

Lord knows
    there are infinite ways to find
    your own way.

V

Longing for Heritage

After I've done the best I can
I somehow feel something is missing

I miss
not having traditions
in my life (any longer)
even the Friday Sabbath
dinners.
Form and rituals
however boring
offer a sense
of security and continuity.

I wonder
sometimes
if I will become
religious
out of despair
or insecurity
however much
I want to embrace
God
Out of love.

Erev Hanukkah

VI

Fortunately Not Every Day Is Important

Alone
    feeling sorry for
    the plants
    unwatered
    like my love
    in the Fall of
    life

I

    seek the sun
    among withered flowers
    and brief encounters
    where friendship lingers
    not for long.
    I am loved
    not enough to still the
    Exile. I lit two candles to

Find

    The way. No one noticed
    What is a way to a
    Jewish holiday?
    Then

God

    responded, somewhat impatiently
    I thought,
    "For Heaven's Sake, Water the
    Plants, And Get On With It."

VII

I believe
in only two Miracles

The first
    recognition that you are unique.
    The miracle surfaces
  when you stop comparing yourself
  with anybody else.
The second
    the coming of the Messiah.

Creative Infidelity
On Being Happy In An Unhappy World

by Sol Gordon

How can I be happy if I have public memories like

> The Spanish Civil War
> The Second World War
> The Soviet carnage
> The American black experience

and for me the special disasters

> The Holocaust
> Vietnam
> The assassination of heroic possibilities
> The Yom Kippur War

and private tragedies

> Bill, is it true that only the good die young?
> J., will you ever love me? Now I know (too late?) that
> you have, in your own sad way.

Mom and Dad, you would have been so proud
   had you lived nine more years!
And Bobby, not even 30 years old - why
   did you blow your brains out?
   And David, such a joy of a boy—not yet 18—and dead.

And yet

   I'm mainly happy

because

   I believe

life is not a meaning but an opportunity.

   life is not often
     harmonious
     congruent
     rational
     or heroic (for me)

All really pleasurable experiences are

   of brief duration
   repeatable from time to time
   but brief

          love
          orgasm
          sunsets

I love many people

   in love with only one I can
   count on always

I love to do many things

   (and I have the money for everything
   I want that costs money)

I'm clever

   enough to play with clever notions

like

   cheap is expensive
   relevance is boring
   try hard to stand for something. Otherwise,
   you'll fall for anything.
   if you are bored, you are boring to be with
   all thoughts are normal (guilt is the energy
     for obsessive unacceptable thoughts)

I know what to do when I'm depressed

   I learn something new

I'm a big proponent of the "Zug a gut wort" theory (Yiddish for "say a good word"). I'm nice to most people, even people I don't know or like.

I have little patience for people who claim they are objective, fair, or nondirective.

Sometimes

> I'm sad for this world
> and for my lack of heroic possibilities

But

> I do the best I can
> I give humorous talks and write books

Yet,

> I sacrifice little
> I eat all my meals enjoyably
>   without thinking much about Ethiopia
> I give to charities
> I'm politically aware, socially right
> I select and don't settle
> I make new friends

And these are the 68* "things" I enjoy the most:

1. Daydream the destruction of the forces of evil

2. Nightdream the current love of my life

3. A New York City weekend with my wife

   (a) gourmet meal
   (b) ballet
   (c) topped off by the Sunday edition of *The New York Times* in the bathtub of a luxurious hotel.

4. Marc Chagall

5. Bittersweet stories and chocolate

6. Mozart

7. Lots of cities

   > Jerusalem
   > Copenhagen
   > Florence
   > Bruges
   > to say nothing of San Francisco and Rome

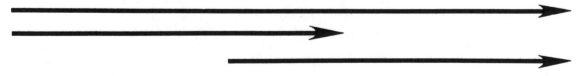

*If we want to grow up, and not old, we should be able to intensely enjoy at least the number of things equal to our age.

8. Lots of museums

   The Met, Hermitage, MOMA, Frick,
   Prado, Uffizi, Tate, Gardiner
   and would you believe the one in Philadelphia?

9. Lynd Ward and Kathe Köllwitz

10. Starting a new Iris Murdoch novel on my way to California and finishing it on my way back

11. Having a marvelously funny, reminiscent day with one of my friends, taking in a walk, a scenic meal, and sometimes a deeply agonizing but liberating philosophic dialogue

12. The joy of Owen Dodson, one of America's finest black poets

13. *Harold and Maude,* all of Charles Chaplin's and about 31 films in my life with *Les Enfants du Paradis* as the supreme triumph

14. When someone says to me, "Oh, so you are Sol Gordon"

15. Saying "no" when someone asks, "Can I trust you?"

16. Sad, serious plays like *A Long Day's Journey Into Night*

17. The boredom of Andy Warhol

18. The agony and music of my Judaism

19. Public television: *Upstairs, Downstairs*

20. Elie Wiesel, because he reminds me of who I am

21. Making fun of people who are "so busy" but accomplish little

22. Uninterrupted classical music

23. Sending out vibrations to perfect strangers and then asking if they got them. Some do and we become friends

24. Virgil Thompson and Gertrude Stein's *Four Saints in Three Acts*—even though I seem to be the only one left who adores it (Pigeons on the Grass, Alas)

25. Risking intimacy quickly

26. People whose "work" I admire, but I suspect we wouldn't hit it off if we met: Leonard Cohen, Sidney Lumet, Ralph Nader, Marlon Brando, Gloria Steinem, Bella Abzug, Ingmar Bergman, Hugh Prather, and Woody Allen

27. Feeling younger now than I felt 27 years ago

28. Being alone sometimes

29. Nature, but not too much of it at a time

30. Walks

31. Reading slowly the good novelists, like Mann, Camus, Thomas Wolfe, Dostoyevsky, Herman Melville, Romain Rolland, Virginia Woolf, I. J. Singer and, would you believe, Sholem Asch

32. The big, beautiful house we live in although everyone says it's too big for the two of us

33. The excitement of the opera or the ballet at the Met

34. The paintings of the now-known Fasanella and the still-unknown Howard Siskowitz, Rita Fecher, and Peter Siegel

35. Imagining the surprise of everybody when they discover who I really am

36. Fantasizing the number one or two spot for my still unpublished "Sex Is" book on *The New York Times* best sellers list

37. Realizing as an ultra busy person I have the time for everything I want to do

38. Convincing people I read minds

39. Playing with remedial educators with my slogan, "Don't try to unblock a block with a block"

40. The Tchaikovsky Trio in A Minor, op. 50 with Arthur, Jascha and Gregor

41. Britten's Serenade for Tenor (Peter Pears) Horn and Strings

42. T. S. Eliot's *Let us go you and I*

43. Being warm and intimate with people I care about

44. Remembering my mother's expressions like, "How can good food be bad for you?"

45. The furniture of George Nakashima

46. Sex

47. I love teaching, influencing, intellectualizing (especially with people who appreciate my sense of humor)

48. I love being influenced by and learning from people who are really smart and who don't take themselves too seriously

49. I enjoy introducing to new friends my ideas and experiences such as the ballet and things Jewish

50. When asked to do something I don't want to do with the incentive "You'll make a lot of money"—I revel in responding, "I'm not interested. I'm independently wealthy"

51. Not wasting my *Time* by reading it in the john

52. Hundertwasser, a painter after my own fantasy

53. *The Wonder Years*

54. Our visit to Japan, especially Kyoto

55. *Ragtime* and *The World According to Garp*

56. Great theatrical experiences like *Equus, Children of a Lesser God,* and *For Colored Girls Who Have Considered Suicide When the Rainbow Is Enuf*

57. Martin Buber, who taught me about the miracle of uniqueness.

58. Announcing the discovery of a new therapeutic technique—works every time. It is called *mitzvah* therapy. In this context the Hebrew *mitzvah* means a good deed. It's simple—"one *mitzvah* leads to another."

59. The secret of wisdom is kindness.

60. Jewish Scripture says, "He who saves one life saves the world entire."

61, 62.   Milan Kundera's *The Book of Laughter and Forgetting* and *The Unbearable Lightness of Being.*

63, 64, 65.   Becoming a missionary with the message that knowledge isn't harmful.

66, 67, 68.   Acts of kindness.

✡ ✡ ✡ ✡ ELEVEN LAST MINUTE SURVIVAL* IDEAS ✡ ✡ ✡ ✡

1 Risk intimacy by telling people about yourself. You thus become vulnerable to being abused and rejected, embraced and accepted.

2 If you can't be somebody you want to be, at least don't be somebody you don't want to be.

3 If you have a tendency to be self-deprecating, don't tell anyone. It's really boring to be with anyone who is down on him/herself.

4 If you have advice to give, don't expect anyone to follow it easily (or at all). When was the last time someone told you "not to worry" and you stopped worrying?

5 If you do something wrong, you should feel guilty. Mature guilt is organizing, but not long-lasting. You will either make amends or you won't do it again.

6 If you feel guilty about something that doesn't make sense—like having "evil" thoughts—your guilt will disorganize you and be the energy for repeating the unacceptable thoughts (obsessions) or behavior (compulsions) over and over again.

7 If your love for another person is mature, it will energize you and contribute to your feeling optimistic about yourself. If your love is immature it will exhaust you, generate feelings of depression, anger and jealousy.

8 If you want to change a *behavior* of yours (for example, talking too much or not enough) your initial efforts to change must be forced or mechanical. You are trying to counteract unacceptable behavior which has become a habit—in a sense a spontaneous, "natural" response to tension. Upon forcing an alternate response (e.g. not talking so much) you will be "rewarded" by enormous rushes of anxiety. If you are able to tolerate the "mechanical" changes and the related tension, you will be able to change to a more acceptable "habit." (Number eight is heavy; read it over.)

9 If you are intolerant of someone else's behavior—like a person who boasts a lot but is not hurting you—you are reacting to something about yourself that you don't like.

10 The process of not doing what you are supposed to do is much more tiring than doing and getting the most boring tasks over with. The ultimate creative busyness is when you have time for almost everything you want to do.

11 The criticism of someone you don't respect should have no impact on you. Life is too precious for you to be offended by or react to anybody's ridicule. Remember too, not everything you say or they say is important. Select, don't settle.

*We mean survival—not salvation.

149

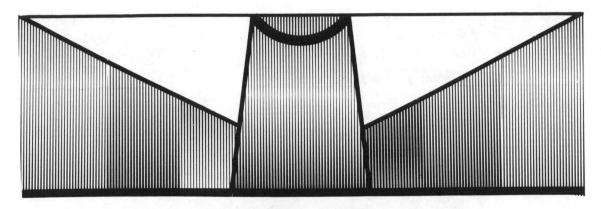

AUT INVENIAM
VIAM
AUT FACIAM—

I SHALL EITHER
FIND A WAY
OR MAKE ONE

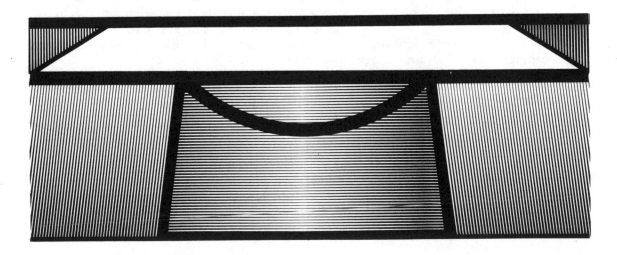